Curry
BIBLE

Curry
BIBLE

Exotic and fragrant curries

Mridula Baljekar

Love Food ® is an imprint of Parragon Books Ltd

Parragon
Queen Street House
4 Queen Street
Bath BA1 1HE, UK

ISBN: 978-1-4075-7462-2

Printed in China

Contributing author: Mridula Baljekar
Additional recipes by Beverly LeBlanc, Judy Williams and Corinne Trang
Photography by Mike Cooper
Cover photography by Clive Streeter
Food styling by Sumi Glass, Carole Handslip and Lincoln Jefferson
Internal design by Sarah Edwards

Notes for the Reader

This book uses both metric and imperial measurements. Follow the same units of measurement throughout; do not mix metric and imperial. All spoon measurements are level: teaspoons are assumed to be 5 ml, and tablespoons are assumed to be 15 ml. Unless otherwise stated, milk is assumed to be full fat, eggs and individual vegetables are medium, and pepper is freshly ground black pepper.

The times given are an approximate guide only. Preparation times differ according to the techniques used by different people and the cooking times may also vary from those given. Optional ingredients, variations or serving suggestions have not been included in the calculations.

Recipes using raw or very lightly cooked eggs should be avoided by infants, the elderly, pregnant women, convalescents and anyone suffering from an illness. Pregnant and breastfeeding women are advised to avoid eating peanuts and peanut products. Sufferers from nut allergies should be aware that some of the ready-made ingredients used in the recipes in this book may contain nuts. Always check the packaging before use.

Contents

Introduction

Curries are popular the world over because of
the exciting colours, varied textures and complex
flavours produced by the spices. Some of the world's
most exotic curries are found in India and South
East Asia. These regions offer delectable curries
with distinctly different cooking styles, which
are directly influenced by internal and external
factors prevalent in each country. The cuisines of
the subcontinent of India and the south-east Asian countries, such as Burma,
Malaysia, Indonesia and Vietnam, have been influenced by invasion of foreign
powers and their subsequent rule. The mouth-watering curries eaten in these
countries have tingled the taste buds of the world and curry has now become a
firm favourite in almost every corner of the globe. But what exactly is a 'curry'?
There is more than one explanation of the meaning of the word: one source
suggests that it originates from the South Indian language Tamil in which
curry (spelt 'kaari') means a spicy sauce. It is also believed that, during the
British Raj, the spelling of 'kaari' was changed to 'curry'. However, more recent
research shows that the history of the curry can be traced back to the dawn
of time. Archaeological evidence found in Mesopotamia (present-day Iraq)
mentions a meat dish with a spicy sauce that could have been the first recorded
curry. Today, however, there is no doubt that the word 'curry' has become
synonymous with a spicy sauce in which meat, poultry, fish or vegetables
are cooked.

The first record of India's spice wealth goes back to as early as AD 629, when the Chinese traveller Huien Tsang passed through India. It was indeed the lure of spices that attracted a host of foreign invaders to India. Nomadic tribes, traders and pilgrims entered India and their cooking styles became a part of the colourful cuisine of the country.

The geographical position of South East Asia, on the far side of India's holy river, the Ganges, has been described as Farther India. The diverse climatic and geographical conditions of this region have given rise to a wide range of crops resulting in a diverse cuisine. A breathtaking range of food, with very clear regional differences, makes Asian cuisine a multidimensional tapestry that is as rich as it is colourful and as intoxicating as it is inimitable. It reflects the heritage of the people of its land and the influences of historical and cultural developments and religious beliefs.

Asian curries, especially Indian, today have gained global recognition. The diverse nature of the curries of Asia has been extended further in other countries around the world because of the need to combine spices with locally grown ingredients. In recent years the appeal of spices has grown at an astonishing rate throughout the world. The exquisite flavours of high-quality spices grown in India have added a new dimension to international cuisine. Today India is rightly described as the 'spice bowl of the world'.

The Spice Route

Spices have been used for thousands of years in Asia, Arabia and the Mediterranean. In 332 BC, Alexander the Great founded Alexandria, which soon became the meeting point for spice merchants from East and West.

The Greeks used several routes to bring spices from the East. History has it that the oldest route started from the Malabar Coast in southern India. This route then went around the coast of Arabia, and up the Red Sea into the Mediterranean region. It became the main trade route between Asia and Europe for many years. At the same time, an overland trading route, running from Europe through Asia Minor into Asia and leading right up to China, was often used by merchants for trading in silk and spices.

When initially the Portuguese, and finally the British, established their empire in India, they acquired control of the Asian maritime routes. This diminished the importance of the 'Spice Route', but spices still played a far-reaching and influential role in the economies of many countries.

India and South East Asia have had the magical and mysterious power to attract visitors and traders since ancient times. The Arabs, English, Dutch, Portuguese and Spanish came to India and South East Asia lured by spices. Afghanistan on the northern border of India and the paradise islands of Indonesia in the south have enticed foreign traders over the centuries.

Spices lie at the heart of the strong resemblance between the cooking styles of India and South East Asia. It is also the spices that set apart the culinary styles of these regions. For instance, the cuisine of south India, with its use of coconut and curry leaves, is strikingly similar to that of South East Asia, where coconut is used extensively with kaffir lime leaves and lemon grass to add extra zest. In Malaysian cuisine one sees a strong Indian influence contributed by the commercial community of India who migrated to this region several centuries ago. The evidence of European influences in the cuisine of Vietnam and the islands

of the Philippines is strong even today. Vietnamese cuisine draws influences from the French, while the Philippines show a strong tendency towards Spanish cooking styles. Thailand, on the other hand, boasts a totally indigenous style of cooking as the country has been free from colonization.

The influence of spices in the West has reached an astonishing level in recent years. As well as in kitchens and homes, spicy food is also finding its way to the supermarket shelves in Europe, the United States, Canada, Australia, Africa and many other countries. International trade in spices has enjoyed phenomenal growth in recent years and well over 500,000 tonnes, exceeding a value of US$1,500 million, is exported globally by India.

A recent publication shows that the first 'curry house' opened in Britain in 1809. Today there are 9,000 Indian restaurants in Britain and numerous south-east Asian restaurants are also enjoying huge popularity. Supermarket shelves are packed full of Asian curry dishes. In recent years the taste for curry has spread across Europe and Asian restaurants have started appearing in major European cities. Supermarkets are also very well stocked with Asian ingredients and making an authentic curry at home has become easier than ever. This trend has travelled across the Atlantic and many parts of the United States and Canada are now enjoying curries in restaurants and in the form of ready meals from the supermarkets. The exotic curries of Asia have become the choice for dinner parties because they provide interest and excitement with their exquisite tastes, flavours and appetizing appearances. It is evident that the curry craze will continue to grow and the spices of Asia will continue to inspire palates worldwide.

Essential curry ingredients

Aniseed

Anise is native to India and looks rather like a celery seed. It is related to caraway and cumin, but the flavour is more akin to that of thyme. Anise aids digestion.

Asafoetida

Obtained from the resinous gum of a tropical plant, asafoetida can be bought from Asian stores in block or powder form. It should be used sparingly because of its strong flavour.

Bay leaf

Bay leaves used in curries are different from those used in the West. Asian bay leaves come from the cassia tree, whereas the Western ones are obtained from sweet bay laurel. Western bay leaves are a popular substitute, as the Asian ones are rarely available in the West.

Cardamom

Cardamom has been used in Asian cooking since ancient times. Whole cardamom pods are used to flavour rice and different types of sauces. Ground cardamom, used in many desserts and drinks, can be bought from most Asian stores, but grinding small quantities at home using a coffee mill will produce better flavours.

Chillies, fresh

Chillies come in different sizes, strengths and colours. Generally, the small thin ones are hot while the large fleshy ones tend to be milder. Most of the heat is in the seeds and the membrane. It is best to remove them if you prefer a milder flavour.

Chilli powder

When fresh green chillies are ripe, they turn a rich red. These are dried to obtain dried red chillies. Chilli powder is made by finely grinding dried red chillies. Crushed dried chillies are also made by grinding dried red chillies to a coarse texture. These are sold in Asian stores.

Cinnamon

One of the oldest spices, cinnamon is obtained from the dried bark of a tropical plant related to the laurel family. It has a warm flavour and is used in both savoury and sweet dishes.

Cloves

Cloves are the unripened dried buds of a southern Asian evergreen tree. They have a strong distinctive flavour and are used both whole and ground. Clove oil is used to remedy toothache.

Coconut

Coconut milk is made by grating, blending and squeezing the juice from coconut flesh. The first extraction is thicker and the second, made from the remaining blended coconut by soaking it in water, is thinner. The second extraction can be boiled for a longer time than the first, which releases too much of the oil when boiled. Canned coconut milk is an ideal substitute for the second extraction.

Creamed coconut comes in a block and is readily available in supermarkets. It can be used to replace the first extraction from a fresh coconut and should be added towards the end of cooking time.

Desiccated coconut is grated fresh coconut that has been dried to prolong its shelf life. It is used in both sweet and savoury dishes, including a variety of desserts and sweetmeats. Coconut milk can be made by soaking desiccated coconut in hot milk and blending it in an electric blender.

Coriander, fresh

The fresh leaves of the coriander plant are widely used in Asian cuisine for flavouring as well as garnishing. They also form the basis of many chutneys and pastes.

Coriander, seed

The fruit produced by the mature coriander plant is the seed that is used as a spice. Its sweet, mellow flavour is very important in south-east Asian curries.

Cumin

Cumin is used either whole or ground. It has a warm and assertive taste. The whole seeds are used to flavour the oil for many vegetarian dishes and the ground version is used in curries. There are two varieties: black and white. Each has its own distinct flavour and one cannot be substituted for the other. Black cumin is sometimes confused with caraway.

Curry leaves

A hallmark of southern Indian cooking, these have an assertive flavour. Fresh and dried versions are sold in Asian shops. Dried ones can be stored in an airtight jar and the fresh ones can be frozen and used when required.

Curry powder and curry pastes

Curry powder is a British invention that was created in southern India and exported to Britain when the British returned home at the end of the Raj. It is produced by blending several spices together, making it easier to create curries. In India, spices are individually blended during cooking and curry powder is never used. It is, however, a popular ingredient in south-east Asian curries.

Curry pastes are commonly used in south-east Asian cooking and are made in the similar way to curry powder, but oil is added to the powdered spices in order to make it into a paste. This also helps to preserve the wet spice blend. Wet spice blends, cooked out correctly, impart a superior flavour. The tradition of curry pastes perhaps originated from the traditional Indian and south-east Asian practice of grinding spices in a grinding stone with water added to them.

Fennel seeds

These have a taste similar to that of anise. They have been used in curries since ancient times. In India, fennel is used as a breath freshener.

Fenugreek

A strong and aromatic herb, fenugreek is cultivated in India and Pakistan, but is native to the Mediterranean region. The fresh leaves are cooked like spinach in a variety of ways, and they are dried and used in smaller quantities to flavour meat and poultry dishes. Fenugreek seeds are used to flavour vegetables, lentils and some fish dishes. They have a distinctive flavour and powerful taste, and should be used only in minute quantities.

Fish sauce

Fish sauce is one of the most commonly used ingredients in south-east Asian cooking, especially Thailand, where it is known as *nam pla*. It is made from anchovies packed with liquid salt; the liquid that is eventually released by the fish is collected and sold as fish sauce. It enhances the overall flavours of south-east Asian curries.

Garam masala

The word *garam* means 'heat' and *masala* refers to the blending of different spices. They are believed to create body heat. The basic ingredients are cinnamon, cardamom, cloves and black pepper. Other spices are added to these, according to preference.

Garlic

Fresh garlic is an integral part of Asian cooking. Dried flakes, powder and garlic salt cannot create the same authentic flavour. It is always used crushed, minced or puréed. Garlic is beneficial in reducing the level of cholesterol in the blood and its antiseptic properties aid the digestive system.

To make garlic purée, peel a good quantity (at least 6 large bulbs) of garlic and purée the cloves in a blender. To store in the refrigerator for immediate use, preserve the purée in cooking oil and store in an airtight jar. This will keep for 3–4 weeks. Alternatively, divide into small portions, freeze and use as required. You can, of course, buy ready-made garlic purée, but the home-made version has a superior flavour.

Ghee

Ghee has a rich and distinctive flavour and is used liberally in Mogul food. There are two types of ghee: pure butterfat ghee and vegetable ghee. Butterfat ghee is made from unsalted butter and vegetable ghee from vegetable shortening. Ghee can be heated to a high temperature without burning. Both types of ghee are available from Indian stores and larger supermarkets. Unsalted butter can be used in some dishes, but cannot be heated to the same temperature.

Ginger

Like garlic, fresh root ginger is vital in making curries. Ginger has a warm, woody aroma. On the medicinal side, ginger is believed to improve circulation of the blood and reduce acidity in the stomach. Dry ginger is used in some dishes, though not in curries.

To make ginger purée, peel the ginger using a potato peeler or scrape off the skin with a small sharp knife. Once peeled, chop roughly and purée in a blender. To store in the refrigerator for immediate use, preserve the purée in cooking oil and store in an airtight jar. This will keep for 3–4 weeks. Alternatively, divide into small portions, freeze and use as required.

If you buy ready-made ginger purée, make sure it is preserved in oil and not citric acid, which tends to impair the flavour.

Galangal

This comes in two varieties: greater galangal, also known as Laos ginger or Thai ginger, and lesser galangal. The former is more widely available and is an essential ingredient in most south-east Asian curries, especially in Thailand. It has a creamy white flesh with a pine-like aroma. Lesser galangal, with its orange-tinged flesh, has a stronger and hotter flavour.

Lemon grass

Lemon grass has an intensely lemony flavour without the acidity of the fruit. It is widely used in south-east Asian curries, soups, curry pastes and pickles. Dried and ground lemon grass, known as 'serai powder', makes a good alternative to fresh. Fresh lemon grass can be frozen successfully.

Limes/kaffir lime leaves

Kaffir limes are widely used throughout south-east Asia. They lend an intense lemony bouquet to curries and curry pastes. The leaves can be used whole or finely shredded, and the latter method imparts a superior flavour. They can be frozen and used as required.

Mustard seeds

Mustard seeds are an essential ingredient in vegetarian cooking. Black and brown mustard seeds are the ones most commonly used, with the white ones being reserved for making pickles. Black and brown seeds lend a nutty flavour to the dish.

Nigella seeds

These tiny black seeds are also known as onion seeds because of their striking resemblance. The seeds are used whole for flavouring vegetables, pickles, breads and snacks.

Palm sugar

This dark, coarse and unrefined sugar is made from the sap of the coconut palm tree. It is also referred to as jaggery. It has a sweet wine-like flavour and usually comes in the form of a solid cake with a crumbly texture.

Peppercorns

Fresh green berries are dried in the sun to obtain black pepper. Green berries come from the pepper vine native to the monsoon forests of South West India. Whole black peppercorns will keep well in an airtight jar, but ground black pepper loses its wonderful aromatic flavour very quickly – it best to store whole peppercorns in a pepper mill and grind as needed.

Poppy seeds

The opium poppy, grown mainly in the tropics, produces the best poppy seeds. There are two varieties: white and black. The white seeds are ground and added to curries to give them a nutty flavour. They are also used as a thickener and as a topping for naan.

Rosewater

Rosewater is the diluted essence of a special strain of edible rose, the petals of which are used to garnish Mogul dishes. Rose essence is more concentrated and only a few drops are needed if it is used instead of rose water.

Saffron

The saffron crocus grows extensively in Kashmir in northern India. Around 250,000 stamen of this crocus are needed to produce just 450 g/1 lb of saffron. It is a highly concentrated ingredient and only minute quantities are required to flavour and colour any dish.

Shrimp paste

A popular ingredient in south-east Asian curries, shrimp paste is made from fermented shrimps, or prawns, pounded with salt into a paste. It is also known as 'terasi', 'blachan' and 'balachan' and it has a strong, fishy and salty flavour.

Sesame seeds

These pale seeds have a rich and nutty flavour. They are native to India, which is the largest exporter of sesame oil to the West. They may be sprinkled on naan before baking, ground to a paste and used to thicken sauces, and used with vegetables and some sweet dishes.

Tamarind

Resembling pea pods at first, tamarind turns dark brown with a thin hard outer shell when ripe. The chocolate brown flesh is encased in the shell with seeds, which have to be removed. The flesh is sold dried and has to be soaked in hot water to yield a pulp. Ready-to-use concentrated tamarind pulp or juice is quick and easy to use. Valued for its distinctive flavour, tamarind is added to vegetables, lentils, peas, chutneys and many fish and seafood dishes.

Turmeric

Fresh turmeric rhizomes resemble root ginger, with a beige-brown skin and bright yellow flesh. Fresh turmeric is dried and ground to produce this essential spice, which should be used in carefully measured quantities to prevent a bitter taste.

Essential recipes

1 tbsp coriander seeds
1 tbsp cumin seeds
12 fresh green bird's eye chillies, chopped
5 garlic cloves, chopped
2 lemon grass stalks, chopped
5 fresh kaffir lime leaves, chopped
handful of fresh coriander, chopped
finely grated rind of 1 lime
1 tsp salt
1 tsp black peppercorns, crushed

THAI GREEN CURRY PASTE

Heat a dry frying pan until hot, add the coriander and cumin seeds and cook over a medium–high heat, shaking the frying pan frequently, for 2–3 minutes, or until starting to pop. Put the toasted seeds with all the remaining ingredients in a food processor or small blender and process to a thick, smooth paste. Transfer to a screw-top glass jar and store in the refrigerator for up to a week.

1 tbsp coriander seeds
1 tbsp cumin seeds
12 dried red chillies, chopped
2 shallots, chopped
6 garlic cloves, chopped
2.5-cm/1-inch piece fresh ginger, chopped
2 lemon grass stalks, chopped
4 fresh kaffir lime leaves, chopped
handful of fresh coriander, chopped
finely grated rind of 1 lime
1 tsp salt
1 tsp black peppercorns, crushed

THAI RED CURRY PASTE

Heat a dry frying pan until hot, add the coriander and cumin seeds and cook over a medium–high heat, shaking the frying pan frequently, for 2–3 minutes, or until starting to pop. Put the toasted seeds with all the remaining ingredients in a food processor or small blender and process to a thick, smooth paste. Transfer to a screw-top glass jar and store in the refrigerator for up to a week.

3 small fresh orange or yellow chillies, chopped
3 garlic cloves, chopped
4 shallots, chopped
3 tsp ground turmeric
1 tsp salt
12–15 black peppercorns, crushed
1 lemon grass stalk (white part only), chopped
2.5-cm/1-inch piece fresh ginger, chopped

THAI YELLOW CURRY PASTE

Put all the ingredients in a food processor or small blender and process to a thick, smooth paste. Transfer to a screw-top glass jar and store in the refrigerator for up to a week.

MUSSAMAN CURRY PASTE

4 large dried red chillies
2 tsp shrimp paste
3 shallots, finely chopped
3 garlic cloves, finely chopped
2.5-cm/1-inch piece fresh galangal, chopped
2 lemon grass stalks (white part only), finely chopped
2 cloves
1 tbsp coriander seeds
1 tbsp cumin seeds
seeds from 3 green cardamom pods
1 tsp black peppercorns
1 tsp salt

Cut off and discard the chilli stalks and place the chillies in a bowl. Cover with hot water and soak for 30–45 minutes. Wrap the shrimp paste in foil and grill or dry-fry for 2–3 minutes, turning once or twice. Remove from the grill or frying pan. Dry-fry the shallots, garlic, galangal, lemon grass, cloves and coriander, cumin and cardamom seeds over a low heat, stirring frequently, for 3–4 minutes, until lightly browned. Transfer to a food processor and process until finely ground. Add the chillies and their soaking water and the peppercorns and salt, and process again. Add the shrimp paste and process again to a smooth paste. Transfer to a screw-top glass jar and store in the refrigerator for up to a week.

PENANG CURRY PASTE

8 large dried red chillies
2 tsp shrimp paste
3 shallots, chopped
5-cm/2-inch piece fresh galangal, chopped
8 garlic cloves, chopped
4 tbsp chopped coriander root
3 lemon grass stalks (white part only), chopped
grated rind of 1 lime
1 tbsp fish sauce
2 tbsp vegetable or groundnut oil
1 tsp salt
6 tbsp crunchy peanut butter

Cut off and discard the chilli stalks and place the chillies in a bowl. Cover with hot water and soak for 30–45 minutes. Wrap the shrimp paste in foil and grill or dry-fry for 2–3 minutes, turning once or twice. Put the chillies and their soaking water into a blender or food processor. Add the shrimp paste, shallots, galangal, garlic, coriander root and lemon grass and process until finely chopped. Add the lime rind, fish sauce, oil and salt and process again. Add the peanut butter and process to make a thick paste. Transfer to a screw-top glass jar and store in the refrigerator for up to a week.

GARLIC AND GINGER PASTE

1–2 garlic bulbs, separated into cloves, roughly chopped
large piece fresh ginger, roughly chopped

Put equal weights of garlic and ginger in a food processor or small blender and process to a smooth paste. Transfer to a screw-top glass jar and store in the refrigerator for up to a week.

GARAM MASALA

2 bay leaves, crumbled
2 cinnamon sticks, broken in half
seeds from 8 green cardamom
pods
2 tbsp cumin seeds
1½ tbsp coriander seeds
1½ tsp black peppercorns
1 tsp cloves
¼ tsp ground cloves

Heat a dry frying pan over a high heat until a splash of water 'dances' when it hits the surface. Reduce the heat to medium, add the bay leaves, cinnamon sticks, cardamom seeds, cumin seeds, coriander seeds, peppercorns and cloves and dry-fry, stirring constantly, until the cumin seeds look dark golden brown and you can smell the aromas. Immediately tip the spices out of the pan and leave to cool. Use a spice grinder or pestle and mortar to grind the spices to a fine powder. Stir in the ground cloves. Store in an airtight container for up to 2 months.

GHEE

250 g/9 oz butter

Melt the butter in a large heavy-based saucepan over a medium heat and continue simmering until a thick foam appears on the surface. Continue simmering, uncovered, for 15–20 minutes, or until the foam separates and the milk solids settle on the bottom and the liquid becomes clear and golden.

Meanwhile, line a sieve with a piece of muslin and place the sieve over a bowl. Slowly pour the liquid through the muslin, without disturbing the milk solids at the bottom of the pan. Discard the milk solids.

Leave the ghee to cool, then transfer to a smaller container, cover and chill. Store in the refrigerator for up to 4 weeks.

PANEER

2.2 litres/4 pints milk
6 tbsp lemon juice

Pour the milk into a large heavy-based saucepan over a high heat and bring to the boil. Remove the pan from the heat and stir in the lemon juice. Return the pan to the heat and continue boiling for a further minute, until the curds and whey separate and the liquid is clear.

Remove the pan from the heat and set aside for an hour or so, until the milk is completely cool. Meanwhile, line a sieve with a piece of muslin large enough to hang over the edge and place the sieve over a bowl.

Pour the curds and whey into the muslin, then gather up the edges and squeeze out all the excess moisture.

Use a piece of string to tightly tie the muslin around the curds in a ball. Put the ball in a bowl and place a plate on top. Place a food can on the plate to weigh down the curds, then chill in the refrigerator for at least 12 hours. The curds will press into a compact mass that can be cut. The paneer will keep for up to 3 days in the refrigerator.

Chicken

Chicken Tikka Masala

This Indian dish reputedly started life in London restaurants as a way to use up leftover cooked tandoori chicken. It has now gone full cycle and is prepared in Indian restaurants. The quickest way to make this is to buy cooked tandoori chicken pieces from a supermarket or an Indian take-away. If, however, you want to make your own tandoori chicken, follow the recipe on page 22, then cut the cooked bird into pieces.

SERVES 4-6

400 g/14 oz canned chopped tomatoes

300 ml/10 fl oz double cream

1 cooked tandoori chicken, cut into
    8 pieces

salt and pepper

fresh chopped coriander, to garnish

cooked basmati rice, to serve

TIKKA MASALA

30 g/1 oz ghee or 2 tbsp vegetable or
    groundnut oil

1 large garlic clove, finely chopped

1 fresh red chilli, deseeded and chopped

2 tsp ground cumin

2 tsp ground paprika

½ tsp salt

pepper

To make the tikka masala, melt the ghee in a large frying pan with a lid over a medium heat. Add the garlic and chilli and stir-fry for 1 minute. Stir in the cumin, paprika, salt and pepper to taste and continue stirring for about 30 seconds.

Stir the tomatoes and cream into the pan. Reduce the heat to low and leave the sauce to simmer for about 10 minutes, stirring frequently, until it reduces and thickens.

Meanwhile, remove all the bones and any skin from the tandoori chicken pieces, then cut the meat into bite-sized pieces.

Adjust the seasoning of the sauce, if necessary. Add the chicken pieces to the pan, cover and leave to simmer for 3–5 minutes, until the chicken is heated through. Garnish with coriander and serve with cooked basmati rice.

Tandoori Chicken

Don't expect to duplicate this dish exactly as it is served at your favourite Indian restaurant. That's impossible to do at home – unless you happen to have a tandoor oven in the kitchen – but this recipe comes close, especially if you leave the bird to marinate for a day before cooking. Indian cooks add the bright red-orange colour to tandoori dishes with natural food colourings, such as cochineal. A few drops of synthetic food colouring are a more readily available option for most home cooks.

SERVES 4

1 chicken, weighing 1.5 kg/3 lb 5 oz, skinned
½ lemon
1 tsp salt
30 g/1 oz ghee, melted
fresh coriander sprigs, to garnish
lemon wedges, to serve

TANDOORI MASALA PASTE

1 tbsp garlic and ginger paste
1 tbsp ground paprika
1 tsp ground cinnamon
1 tsp ground cumin
½ tsp ground coriander
¼ tsp chilli powder, ideally Kashmiri chilli powder
pinch of ground cloves
¼ tsp edible red food colouring (optional)
few drops of edible yellow food colouring (optional)
200 ml/7 fl oz natural yogurt

To make the tandoori masala paste, combine the garlic and ginger paste, dry spices and food colouring, if using, in a bowl and stir in the yogurt. You can use the paste now or store it in an airtight container in the refrigerator for up to 3 days.

Use a small knife to make thin cuts all over the chicken. Rub the lemon half over the chicken, then rub the salt into the cuts. Put the chicken in a deep bowl, add the paste and use your hands to rub it all over the bird and into the cuts. Cover the bowl with clingfilm and refrigerate for at least 4 hours, but ideally up to 24 hours.

When you are ready to cook the chicken, preheat the oven to 200°C/400°F/Gas Mark 6. Put the chicken on a rack in a roasting tin, breast-side up, and drizzle over the melted ghee. Roast in the preheated oven for 45 minutes, then quickly remove the bird and roasting tin from the oven and turn the temperature to its highest setting.

Very carefully pour out any fat from the bottom of the roasting tin. Return the chicken to the oven and roast for a further 10–15 minutes, until the juices run clear when you pierce the thigh with a knife and the paste is lightly charred.

Leave to stand for 10 minutes, then cut into pieces. Garnish with coriander sprigs and serve with lemon wedges.

COOK'S TIP

For a quicker version, use chicken breasts, thighs or drumsticks. Marinate as above, preheat the oven to 230°C/450°F/Gas Mark 8 and roast for about 40 minutes.

Pistachio Chicken Korma

It is a common misconception that korma is a mild and creamy dish. In fact, korma is not a dish but one of the several techniques used in Indian cooking. This delectable korma from Delhi has an unusual and irresistible aroma and taste.

SERVES 4

115 g/4 oz shelled pistachio nuts

200 ml/7 fl oz boiling water

good pinch of saffron threads, pounded

2 tbsp hot milk

700 g/1 lb 9 oz skinless, boneless
   chicken breasts or thighs, cut into
   2.5-cm/1-inch cubes

1 tsp salt, or to taste

½ tsp pepper

juice of ½ lemon

55 g/2 oz ghee or unsalted butter

6 green cardamom pods

1 large onion, finely chopped

2 tsp garlic purée

2 tsp ginger purée

1 tbsp ground coriander

½ tsp chilli powder

280 g/10 oz whole milk natural yogurt,
   whisked

150 ml/5 fl oz single cream

2 tbsp rosewater

6–8 white rose petals, washed,
   to garnish

cooked basmati rice and lemon wedges,
   to serve

Soak the pistachio nuts in the boiling water in a heatproof bowl for 20 minutes. Meanwhile, soak the pounded saffron in the hot milk.

Put the chicken in a non-metallic bowl and add the salt, pepper and lemon juice. Rub into the chicken, cover and leave to marinate in the refrigerator for 30 minutes.

Melt the ghee in a medium heavy-based saucepan over a low heat and add the cardamom pods. When they have puffed up, add the onion and increase the heat to medium. Cook, stirring frequently, for 8–9 minutes, until the onion is a pale golden colour.

Add the garlic and ginger purées and cook, stirring frequently, for a further 2–3 minutes. Add the coriander and chilli powder and cook, stirring, for 30 seconds. Add the chicken, increase the heat to medium–high and cook, stirring constantly, for 5–6 minutes, until it changes colour.

Reduce the heat to low and add the yogurt and the saffron and milk mixture. Bring to a slow simmer, cover and cook for 15 minutes. Stir halfway through to ensure that it does not stick to the base of the pan.

Meanwhile, put the pistachio nuts and their soaking water in a blender or food processor and process until smooth. Add to the chicken mixture, followed by the cream. Cover and simmer, stirring occasionally, for a further 15–20 minutes. Stir in the rosewater and remove from the heat. Garnish with the rose petals and serve immediately with cooked basmati rice and lemon wedges.

Kashmiri Chicken

This mild and aromatic Kashmiri dish is delicately flavoured and coloured with saffron threads, grown in the northern region. Chicken thighs are used in this recipe, but any pieces of boneless meat are suitable.

SERVES 4-6

seeds from 8 green cardamom pods

½ tsp coriander seeds

½ tsp cumin seeds

1 cinnamon stick

8 black peppercorns

6 cloves

1 tbsp hot water

½ tsp saffron threads

40 g/1½ oz ghee or 3 tbsp vegetable or groundnut oil

1 large onion, finely chopped

2 tbsp garlic and ginger paste

250 ml/9 fl oz natural yogurt

8 skinless, boneless chicken thighs, sliced

3 tbsp ground almonds

55 g/2 oz blanched pistachio nuts, finely chopped

2 tbsp chopped fresh coriander

2 tbsp chopped fresh mint

salt

toasted flaked almonds, to garnish

Indian bread, to serve

Dry-roast the cardamom seeds in a hot frying pan over a medium–low heat, stirring constantly, until you can smell the aroma. Immediately tip them out of the pan so they don't burn. Repeat with the coriander and cumin seeds, cinnamon, peppercorns and cloves. Put all the spices, except the cinnamon stick, in a spice grinder or mortar and grind to a powder.

Put the hot water and saffron threads in a small bowl and set aside.

Melt the ghee in a flameproof casserole or large frying pan with a tight-fitting lid. Add the onion and cook, stirring occasionally, over a medium–high heat for 5–8 minutes, until it becomes golden brown. Add the garlic and ginger paste and continue stirring for 2 minutes.

Stir in the ground spices and the cinnamon stick. Remove from the heat and mix in the yogurt, a small amount at a time, stirring vigorously with each addition, then return to the heat and continue stirring for 2–3 minutes, until the ghee separates. Add the chicken pieces.

Bring the mixture to the boil, stirring constantly, then reduce the heat to the lowest setting, cover the casserole and simmer for 20 minutes, stirring occasionally and checking that the mixture isn't catching on the base of the pan. If it does start to catch, stir in a few tablespoons of water.

Stir the ground almonds, pistachios, saffron liquid, half the coriander, all the mint and salt to taste into the chicken mixture. Re-cover the pan and continue simmering for about 5 minutes, until the chicken is tender and the sauce is thickened. Sprinkle with the remaining coriander and the flaked almonds and serve with Indian bread.

Butter Chicken

As with Chicken Tikka Masala, the quickest way to prepare this popular Sikh dish is to buy ready-cooked tandoori chicken. Otherwise start with the tandoori chicken recipe on page 22. This is a good party dish, with a rich, creamy sauce that you can make as hot as you like, depending on the amount of chilli powder you include.

SERVES 4-6

1 onion, chopped

1½ tbsp garlic and ginger paste

400 g/14 oz canned chopped tomatoes

¼–½ tsp chilli powder

pinch of sugar

30 g/1 oz ghee or 2 tbsp vegetable or
   groundnut oil

125 ml/4 fl oz water

1 tbsp tomato purée

40 g/1½ oz butter, cut into small pieces

½ tsp garam masala

½ tsp ground cumin

½ tsp ground coriander

1 cooked tandoori chicken,
   cut into 8 pieces

4 tbsp double cream

salt and pepper

chopped cashew nuts and fresh
   coriander sprigs, to garnish

Put the onion and garlic and ginger paste in a food processor, blender or spice grinder and whizz together until a paste forms. Add the tomatoes, chilli powder, sugar and a pinch of salt and whizz again until blended.

Melt the ghee in a wok or large frying pan over a medium–high heat. Add the tomato mixture and water and stir in the tomato purée.

Bring the mixture to the boil, stirring, then reduce the heat to very low and simmer for 5 minutes, stirring occasionally, until the sauce thickens.

Stir in half the butter, the garam masala, cumin and coriander. Add the chicken pieces and stir around until they are well coated. Simmer for about 10 minutes longer, or until the chicken is hot. Taste and adjust the seasoning, if necessary.

Lightly beat the cream in a small bowl and stir in several tablespoons of the hot sauce, beating constantly. Stir the cream mixture into the tomato sauce, then add the remaining butter and stir until it melts. Garnish with the chopped cashew nuts and coriander sprigs and serve straight from the pan.

Chicken Biryani

In this dish from the snowy foothills of the Himalayas, the naturally fragrant basmati rice is enhanced with cinnamon, cardamom and star anise, and layered with delicately spiced chicken. It is cooked in a sealed pot to conserve the flavours.

SERVES 4-5

85 g/3 oz whole milk natural yogurt

1 tbsp garlic purée

1 tbsp ginger purée

700 g/1 lb 9 oz skinless, boneless
    chicken thighs

1 tbsp white poppy seeds

2 tsp coriander seeds

½ mace blade

2 bay leaves, torn into small pieces

½ tsp black peppercorns

1 tsp green cardamom seeds

2.5-cm/1-inch piece cinnamon stick,
    broken up

4 cloves

55 g/2 oz ghee or unsalted butter

1 large onion, finely sliced

1½ tsp salt, or to taste

RICE

pinch of saffron threads, pounded

2 tbsp hot milk

1½ tsp salt

2 x 5-cm/2-inch cinnamon sticks

3 star anise

2 bay leaves, crumbled

4 cloves

4 green cardamom pods, bruised

450 g/1 lb basmati rice, washed

TO GARNISH

2 tbsp sunflower oil

1 onion, finely sliced

Put the yogurt and garlic and ginger purées in a bowl and beat together with a fork until thoroughly blended. Put the chicken in a non-metallic bowl, add the yogurt mixture and mix until well blended. Cover and leave to marinate in the refrigerator for 2 hours.

Grind the next 8 ingredients (all the seeds and spices) to a fine powder in a coffee grinder and set aside. In a flameproof casserole large enough to hold the chicken and the rice together, melt the ghee over a medium heat, add the onion and cook, stirring frequently, for 8–10 minutes, until a medium brown colour. Reduce the heat to low, add the ground ingredients and cook, stirring, for 2–3 minutes. Add the marinated chicken and salt and cook, stirring, for 2 minutes. Turn off the heat and keep the chicken covered.

To make the rice, soak the pounded saffron in the hot milk and set aside to soak for 20 minutes. Preheat the oven to 180°C/350°F/Gas Mark 4. Bring a large saucepan of water to the boil and add the salt and spices. Add the rice, return to the boil and boil steadily for 2 minutes. Drain the rice, reserving the whole spices, and pile on top of the chicken. Pour the saffron and milk over the rice.

Soak a piece of greaseproof paper large enough to cover the top of the rice fully and squeeze out the excess water. Lay on top of the rice. Soak a clean tea towel, wring out and lay loosely on top of the greaseproof paper. Cover the casserole with a piece of foil. It is important to cover the rice in this way to contain all the steam inside the casserole, as the biryani cooks entirely in the vapour created inside the casserole. Put the lid on top and cook in the centre of the preheated oven for 1 hour. Turn off the oven and leave the rice to stand inside for 30 minutes.

Meanwhile, heat the oil for the garnish in a small saucepan over a medium heat, add the onion and cook, stirring, for 12–15 minutes, until browned.

Transfer the biryani to a serving dish and garnish with the fried onions.

31

Chicken Dopiaza

The meaning of dopiaza *remains controversial. It is widely believed to mean a dish with twice the normal amount of onions, but connoisseurs of Mogul food argue that it is a Mogul term meaning any meat or poultry cooked with vegetables.*

SERVES 4

700 g/1 lb 9 oz skinless, boneless
   chicken breasts or thighs

juice of ½ lemon

1 tsp salt, or to taste

5 tbsp sunflower or olive oil

2 large onions, roughly chopped

5 large garlic cloves, roughly chopped

2.5-cm/1-inch piece fresh ginger, roughly
   chopped

2 tbsp whole milk natural yogurt

2.5-cm/1-inch piece cinnamon stick,
   halved

4 green cardamom pods, bruised

4 cloves

½ tsp black peppercorns

½ tsp ground turmeric

½–1 tsp chilli powder

1 tsp ground coriander

4 tbsp passata

150 ml/5 fl oz warm water

½ tsp granulated sugar

8 shallots, halved

1 tsp garam masala

2 tbsp chopped fresh coriander leaves

1 tomato, chopped

Indian bread, to serve

Cut the chicken into 2.5-cm/1-inch cubes and put in a non-metallic bowl. Add the lemon juice and half the salt and rub well into the chicken. Cover and leave to marinate in the refrigerator for 20 minutes.

Heat 1 tablespoon of the oil in a small saucepan over a medium heat, add the onions, garlic and ginger and cook, stirring frequently, for 4–5 minutes. Remove from the heat and leave to cool slightly. Transfer the ingredients to a blender or food processor, add the yogurt and blend to a purée.

Heat 3 tablespoons of the remaining oil in a medium heavy-based saucepan over a low heat, add the cinnamon stick, cardamom pods, cloves and peppercorns and cook, stirring, for 25–30 seconds. Add the puréed ingredients, increase the heat to medium and cook, stirring frequently, for 5 minutes.

Add the turmeric, chilli powder and ground coriander and cook, stirring, for 2 minutes.

Add the passata and cook, stirring, for 3 minutes. Increase the heat slightly, then add the marinated chicken and cook, stirring, until it changes colour. Add the warm water, the remaining salt and the sugar. Bring to the boil, then reduce the heat to low, cover and cook for 10 minutes. Remove the lid and cook, uncovered, for a further 10 minutes, or until the sauce thickens.

Meanwhile, heat the remaining 1 tablespoon of oil in a small saucepan, add the shallots and stir-fry until browned and separated. Add the garam masala and cook, stirring, for 30 seconds. Stir the shallot mixture into the curry and simmer for 2 minutes. Stir in the fresh coriander and chopped tomato and remove from the heat. Serve immediately with Indian bread.

Chicken Jalfrezi

The popular jalfrezi curry was created during the British Raj to use up cold cooked meat. This recipe comes from Kolkata (previously Calcutta), where jalfrezi was served frequently to the members of the East India Company.

SERVES 4

700 g/1 lb 9 oz skinless, boneless
  chicken breasts or thighs

juice of ½ lemon

1 tsp salt, or to taste

5 tbsp sunflower or olive oil

1 large onion, finely chopped

2 tsp garlic purée

2 tsp ginger purée

½ tsp ground turmeric

1 tsp ground cumin

2 tsp ground coriander

½–1 tsp chilli powder

150 g/5½ oz canned chopped tomatoes

150 ml/5 fl oz warm water

1 large garlic clove, finely chopped

1 small or ½ large red pepper, deseeded
  and cut into 2.5-cm/1-inch pieces

1 small or ½ large green pepper,
  deseeded and cut into 2.5-cm/
  1-inch pieces

1 tsp garam masala

Indian bread or cooked basmati rice,
  to serve

Cut the chicken into 2.5-cm/1-inch cubes and put in a non-metallic bowl. Add the lemon juice and half the salt and rub well into the chicken. Cover and leave to marinate in the refrigerator for 20 minutes.

Heat 4 tablespoons of the oil in a medium heavy-based saucepan over a medium heat. Add the onion and cook, stirring frequently, for 8–9 minutes, until lightly browned. Add the garlic and ginger pureés and cook, stirring, for 3 minutes. Add the turmeric, cumin, coriander and chilli powder and cook, stirring, for 1 minute. Add the tomatoes and cook for 2–3 minutes, stirring frequently, until the oil separates from the spice paste.

Add the marinated chicken, increase the heat slightly and cook, stirring, until it changes colour. Add the warm water and bring to the boil. Reduce the heat, cover and simmer for 25 minutes.

Heat the remaining 1 tablespoon of oil in a small saucepan or frying pan over a low heat. Add the garlic and cook, stirring frequently, until browned. Add the red and green peppers, increase the heat to medium and stir-fry for 2 minutes, then stir in the garam masala. Fold the pepper mixture into the curry. Remove from the heat and serve immediately with Indian bread or cooked basmati rice.

Creamy Chicken Tikka

There are several versions of this ever-popular dish, and this one is quite special. Grated mild Cheddar cheese and cream are added to the marinade, and the combination of the dairy ingredients has a magical effect in tenderizing the meat.

SERVES 4

700 g/1 lb 9 oz skinless, boneless
   chicken breasts, cut into 2.5-cm/
   1-inch cubes
2 tbsp lemon juice
½ tsp salt, or to taste
125 g/4½ oz whole milk natural yogurt,
   strained, or Greek-style yogurt
3 tbsp double cream
25 g/1 oz mild Cheddar cheese, grated
1 tbsp garlic purée
1 tbsp ginger purée
½–1 tsp chilli powder
½ tsp ground turmeric
½ tsp granulated sugar
1 tbsp gram flour, sifted
1 tsp garam masala
2 tbsp sunflower or olive oil,
   plus 2 tbsp for brushing
3 tbsp melted butter or olive oil
salad and chutney, to serve

Put the chicken in a non-metallic bowl and add the lemon juice and salt. Rub well into the chicken. Cover and leave to marinate in the refrigerator for 20–30 minutes.

Put the yogurt in a separate non-metallic bowl and beat with a fork until smooth. Add all the remaining ingredients, except the melted butter. Beat well until the ingredients are fully incorporated. Add the chicken and mix thoroughly until fully coated with the marinade. Cover and leave to marinate in the refrigerator for 4–6 hours, or overnight. Return to room temperature before cooking.

Preheat the grill to high. Brush 6 metal skewers generously with the remaining 2 tablespoons of oil and thread on the chicken cubes. Brush over any remaining marinade. Place the prepared skewers in a grill pan and grill about 7.5 cm/3 inches below the heat source for 4–5 minutes. Brush generously with the melted butter and cook for a further 1–2 minutes. Turn over and cook for 3–4 minutes, basting frequently with the remaining melted butter.

Balance the skewers over a large saucepan or frying pan and leave to rest for 5–6 minutes before sliding the chicken cubes off the skewers with a knife. Serve with salad and chutney.

Vietnamese Chicken Curry

This Vietnamese curry is delicate in comparison to the more widely known Thai curries. The sweet and savoury broth is based on coconut milk seasoned with Indian curry powder, fish sauce and lemon grass.

SERVES 6

2 lemon grass stalks

50 ml/2 fl oz vegetable oil

3 large garlic cloves, crushed

1 large shallot, thinly sliced

2 tbsp Indian curry powder

700 ml/1¼ pints coconut milk

500 ml/18 fl oz coconut water
 (not coconut milk) or chicken stock

2 tbsp fish sauce

4 fresh red bird's eye chillies or dried red
 Chinese (tien sien) chillies

6 kaffir lime leaves

6 boneless chicken thighs or breasts,
 175–225 g/6–8 oz each, with or
 without skin, cut into 5-cm/2-inch
 pieces

1 large white yam or sweet potato,
 peeled and cut into 2.5-cm/1-inch
 chunks

2 Asian aubergines, cut into 2.5-cm/
 1-inch pieces

250 g/9 oz green beans, trimmed

2 carrots, peeled and cut diagonally into
 1 cm/½ inch thick pieces

fresh Thai basil sprigs, to garnish

cooked jasmine rice, to serve

Discard the bruised leaves and root ends of the lemon grass stalks, then cut 15–20 cm/6–8 inches of the lower stalks into paper-thin slices.

Heat the oil in a large saucepan over a high heat, then add the garlic and shallot and stir-fry for 5 minutes, or until golden. Add the lemon grass and curry powder and stir-fry for 2 minutes, or until fragrant. Add the coconut milk, coconut water, fish sauce, chillies and lime leaves and bring to the boil. Reduce the heat to low and add the chicken, yam, aubergines, green beans and carrots. Simmer, covered, for 1 hour, or until the chicken and vegetables are tender and the flavours have blended.

Serve garnished with Thai basil sprigs and accompanied by cooked jasmine rice.

Thai Green Chicken Curry

The fiery taste of this fragrant Thai-style curry is mellowed by cooling coconut milk and delicately aromatic herbs. While there are many excellent commercial curry pastes available, it's still worth the effort of making your own (see page 14 for the recipe) – the results will speak for themselves.

SERVES 4

2 tbsp groundnut or sunflower oil

2 tbsp Thai green curry paste

500 g/1 lb 2 oz skinless, boneless
   chicken breasts, cut into cubes

2 kaffir lime leaves, roughly torn

1 lemon grass stalk, finely chopped

225 ml/8 fl oz coconut milk

16 baby aubergines, halved

2 tbsp fish sauce

fresh Thai basil sprigs and thinly sliced
   kaffir lime leaves, to garnish

Heat the oil in a preheated wok or large heavy-based frying pan. Add the curry paste and stir-fry briefly until all the aromas are released.

Add the chicken, lime leaves and lemon grass and stir-fry for 3–4 minutes, until the meat is beginning to colour. Add the coconut milk and aubergines and simmer gently for 8–10 minutes, or until tender.

Stir in the fish sauce and serve immediately, garnished with Thai basil sprigs and lime leaves.

Penang Chicken Curry

This delicious curry dish uses Penang curry paste, a Malaysian-influenced paste that is very similar to Thai red curry paste except that it contains peanuts (see page 15 for the recipe).

SERVES 4

1 tbsp vegetable or groundnut oil

2 red onions, sliced

2 tbsp Penang curry paste

400 ml/14 fl oz coconut milk

150 ml/5 fl oz chicken stock

4 kaffir lime leaves, roughly torn

1 lemon grass stalk, finely chopped

6 skinless, boneless chicken thighs, chopped

1 tbsp fish sauce

2 tbsp Thai soy sauce

1 tsp palm sugar or soft light brown sugar

50 g/1¾ oz unsalted peanuts, roasted and chopped, plus extra to garnish

175 g/6 oz fresh pineapple, roughly chopped

15-cm/6-inch piece cucumber, peeled, deseeded and thickly sliced, plus extra to garnish

Heat the oil in a wok and stir-fry the onions for 1 minute. Add the curry paste and stir-fry for 1–2 minutes.

Pour in the coconut milk and stock. Add the lime leaves and lemon grass and simmer for 1 minute. Add the chicken and gradually bring to the boil. Simmer for 8–10 minutes, until the chicken is tender.

Stir in the fish sauce, soy sauce and sugar and simmer for 1–2 minutes. Stir in the peanuts, pineapple and cucumber and cook for 30 seconds. Serve immediately, sprinkled with extra peanuts and cucumber.

Shredded Chicken & Mixed Mushrooms

Chicken and mushrooms are a magical combination and look fantastic studded with emerald green flecks of parsley. For maximum flavour, make sure to use a mixture of different mushrooms.

SERVES 4

2 tbsp vegetable or groundnut oil

2 skinless, boneless chicken breasts

1 red onion, sliced

2 garlic cloves, finely chopped

2.5-cm/1-inch piece fresh ginger, grated

115 g/4 oz baby button mushrooms

115 g/4 oz shiitake mushrooms, halved

115 g/4 oz chestnut mushrooms, sliced

2–3 tbsp Thai green curry paste

2 tbsp Thai soy sauce

4 tbsp chopped fresh parsley

cooked noodles or rice, to serve

Heat the oil in a wok and cook the chicken on all sides, until lightly browned and cooked through. Remove with a slotted spoon, shred into even-sized pieces and set aside.

Pour off any excess oil, then stir-fry the onion, garlic and ginger for 1–2 minutes, until softened. Add the mushrooms and stir-fry for 2–3 minutes, until they start to brown.

Add the curry paste, soy sauce and shredded chicken to the wok and stir-fry for 1–2 minutes. Stir in the parsley and serve immediately with noodles or rice.

Thai Yellow Chicken Curry

Thai yellow curry paste is the mildest of the Thai curry pastes. This is a healthy version of the traditional Thai curry because it uses natural yogurt rather than coconut milk, which is high in fat.

SERVES 4
SPICE PASTE

6 tbsp Thai yellow curry paste

150 ml/5 fl oz natural yogurt

400 ml/14 fl oz water

handful of fresh coriander, chopped,
   plus extra to garnish

handful of fresh Thai basil leaves,
   shredded, plus extra to garnish

STIR-FRY

2 tbsp vegetable or groundnut oil

2 onions, cut into thin wedges

2 garlic cloves, finely chopped

2 skinless, boneless chicken breasts,
   cut into strips

175 g/6 oz baby corn cobs, halved
   lengthways

To make the spice paste, stir-fry the curry paste in a wok for 2–3 minutes, then stir in the yogurt, water and herbs. Bring to the boil, then simmer for 2–3 minutes.

Meanwhile, heat the oil in a wok and stir-fry the onions and garlic for 2–3 minutes. Add the chicken and corn cobs and stir-fry for 3–4 minutes, until the meat and corn are tender.

Stir in the spice paste and bring to the boil. Simmer for 2–3 minutes, until heated through. Serve immediately, garnished with extra herbs if liked.

Chicken Curry with Fried Noodles

The rice noodles puff up really quickly in hot oil – great entertainment for children to watch at a safe distance – but take care as they are done in a matter of seconds.

SERVES 4

2 tbsp groundnut or vegetable oil, plus extra for deep-frying

4 skinless, boneless chicken breasts, about 115 g/4 oz each, cut into 2.5-cm/1-inch cubes

2 red onions, roughly chopped

5 spring onions, roughly chopped

2 garlic cloves, finely chopped

1 fresh green chilli, deseeded and finely chopped

175 g/6 oz shiitake mushrooms, thickly sliced

2 tbsp Thai green curry paste

400 ml/14 fl oz coconut milk

300 ml/10 fl oz chicken stock

2 fresh kaffir lime leaves

handful of fresh coriander, chopped

handful of fresh chives, snipped

25 g/1 oz dried thin rice noodles

Heat the oil in a preheated wok, add the chicken, in batches, and stir-fry over a medium–high heat for 3–4 minutes, until lightly browned all over. Remove with a slotted spoon, transfer to a plate and set aside.

Add the red onions, spring onions, garlic and chilli to the wok and stir-fry over a medium heat, adding a little more oil if necessary, for 2–3 minutes, until soft but not brown. Add the mushrooms and stir-fry over a high heat for 30 seconds. Return the chicken to the wok.

Add the curry paste, coconut milk, stock and lime leaves and bring gently to the boil, stirring occasionally. Reduce the heat and simmer gently for 4–5 minutes, until the chicken is tender and cooked through. Stir in the coriander and chives.

Meanwhile, heat the oil for deep-frying in a separate wok or deep-sided frying pan to 180–190°C/350–375°F, or until a cube of bread browns in 30 seconds. Divide the noodles into 4 portions and cook, one portion at a time, for about 2 seconds, until puffed up and crisp. Remove with a slotted spoon and drain on kitchen paper.

Serve the curry topped with the crispy noodles.

Wok-cooked Chicken in Tomato & Fenugreek Sauce

A delectable dish from northern India, which is cooked in the Indian-style wok (kadhai) *and is known as* kadhai murgh *in India. The tomato-and-onion-based sauce has the predominant flavour of dried fenugreek leaves (*kasuri methi*), the characteristic ingredient in the cuisine of this region. Chicken thighs have been used here as they have a more succulent taste, but breast meat can be used, if preferred.*

SERVES 4

700 g/1 lb 9 oz skinless, boneless
  chicken thighs, cut into 2.5-cm/1-inch
  cubes
juice of 1 lime
1 tsp salt, or to taste
4 tbsp sunflower or olive oil
1 large onion, finely chopped
2 tsp ginger purée
2 tsp garlic purée
½ tsp ground turmeric
½–1 tsp chilli powder
1 tbsp ground coriander
425 g/15 oz canned chopped tomatoes
125 ml/4 fl oz warm water
1 tbsp dried fenugreek leaves
½ tsp garam masala
2 tbsp chopped fresh coriander leaves
2–4 fresh green chillies
Indian bread, to serve

Place the chicken in a non-metallic bowl and rub in the lime juice and salt. Cover and set aside for 30 minutes.

Heat the oil in a wok or heavy-based frying pan over a medium–high heat. Add the onion and stir-fry for 7–8 minutes, until it begins to colour.

Add the ginger and garlic purées and continue to stir-fry for about a minute. Add the turmeric, chilli powder and ground coriander, then reduce the heat slightly and cook the spices for 25–30 seconds. Add half the tomatoes, stir-fry for 3–4 minutes and add the remaining tomatoes. Continue to cook, stirring, until the tomato juice has evaporated and the oil separates from the spice paste and floats on the surface.

Add the chicken and increase the heat to high. Stir-fry for 4–5 minutes, then add the warm water, reduce the heat to medium–low and cook for 8–10 minutes, or until the sauce has thickened and the chicken is tender.

Add the fenugreek leaves, garam masala, half the coriander leaves and the chillies. Cook for 1–2 minutes, remove from the heat and transfer to a serving plate. Garnish with the remaining coriander and serve with Indian bread.

Cumin-scented Chicken Curry

Cumin-scented chicken, or zeera murgh, *is quick and easy to make and is wonderfully aromatic with cinnamon, cardamom and cloves. The warm and assertive character of cumin plays the central role here, but is in complete harmony with all the other ingredients used.*

SERVES 4

700 g/1 lb 9 oz boneless chicken thighs
  or breasts, cut into 5-cm/2-inch pieces

juice of 1 lime

1 tsp salt, or to taste

3 tbsp sunflower or olive oil

1 tsp cumin seeds

2.5-cm/1-inch piece cinnamon stick

5 green cardamom pods, bruised

4 cloves

1 large onion, finely chopped

2 tsp garlic purée

2 tsp ginger purée

½ tsp ground turmeric

2 tsp ground cumin

½ tsp chilli powder

225 g/8 oz canned chopped tomatoes

1 tbsp tomato purée

½ tsp sugar

225 ml/8 fl oz warm water

½ tsp garam masala

2 tbsp chopped fresh coriander leaves,
  plus extra sprigs to garnish

Indian bread, to serve

Put the chicken in a non-metallic bowl and rub in the lime juice and salt. Cover and set aside for 30 minutes.

Heat the oil in a medium saucepan over a low heat and add the cumin seeds, cinnamon, cardamom and cloves. Let them sizzle for 25–30 seconds, then add the onion. Cook, stirring regularly, for 5 minutes, or until the onion is soft.

Add the garlic and ginger purées and cook for about a minute, then add the turmeric, ground cumin and chilli powder. Add the tomatoes, tomato purée and sugar. Cook over a medium heat, stirring regularly, until the tomatoes reach a paste-like consistency and the oil separates from the paste. Sprinkle over a little water if the mixture sticks to the pan.

Add the chicken and increase the heat to medium–high. Stir until the chicken changes colour, then pour in the warm water. Bring to the boil, reduce the heat to medium–low and cook for 12–15 minutes, or until the sauce has thickened and the chicken is tender.

Stir in the garam masala and chopped coriander. Transfer to a serving dish and garnish with coriander sprigs. Serve with Indian bread.

Chicken in Green Chilli, Mint & Coriander Sauce

When you cook this dish, it will remind you of a summer's garden and its visual appearance will delight you. The emerald green purée of fresh green chillies, mint and coriander embraces the pieces of chicken, which are golden from the turmeric and aromatized with cardamom, cinnamon and nutmeg.

SERVES 4

25 g/1 oz coriander leaves and stalks, roughly chopped

25 g/1 oz fresh spinach, roughly chopped

2.5-cm/1-inch piece fresh ginger, roughly chopped

3 garlic cloves, roughly chopped

2–3 fresh green chillies, roughly chopped

15 g/½ oz fresh mint leaves

1½ tbsp lemon juice

85 g/3 oz thick set natural yogurt

4 tbsp sunflower or olive oil

1 large onion, finely chopped

700 g/1 lb 9 oz skinless chicken thighs or breasts, cut into 2.5-cm/1-inch cubes

1 tsp ground turmeric

½ tsp sugar

salt

1 small tomato, deseeded and cut into julienne strips, to garnish

cooked basmati rice, to serve

Place the coriander, spinach, ginger, garlic, chillies, mint, lemon juice and ½ teaspoon of salt in a food processor or blender and process to a smooth purée. Add a little water, if necessary, to facilitate blade movement in a blender. Remove and set aside.

Whisk the yogurt until smooth (this is important as the yogurt will curdle otherwise) and set aside.

Heat the oil in a medium saucepan and cook the onion for 5–6 minutes, stirring regularly, until soft.

Add the chicken and stir-fry over a medium–high heat for 2–3 minutes, until the meat turns opaque. Add the turmeric, sugar and salt to taste and stir-fry for a further 2 minutes, then reduce the heat to medium and add half the yogurt. Cook for 1 minute and add the remaining yogurt, then continue cooking over a medium heat until the yogurt resembles a thick batter and the oil is visible.

Add the puréed ingredients and cook for 4–5 minutes, stirring constantly. Remove from the heat and garnish with the strips of tomato. Serve with cooked basmati rice.

Fried Chilli Chicken

This recipe, known as ayam goreng berlada, *is from the fabulous range of light, fragrant and aromatic dishes cooked in Malaysia. Influenced by India, China, Indonesia and other neighbouring countries, Malaysia today offers a delightful melange of cross-cultural cuisine. This is a simple but superb recipe in which the chicken is cooked in a paste made of only four fresh spices with a light touch of turmeric.*

SERVES 4

750 g/1 lb 10 oz chicken thighs

3 tbsp lemon juice

1 tsp salt, or to taste

5 large garlic cloves, roughly chopped

5-cm/2-inch piece fresh ginger, roughly chopped

1 medium onion, roughly chopped

2 fresh red chillies, roughly chopped

4 tbsp groundnut oil

1 tsp ground turmeric

½ tsp chilli powder

150 ml/5 fl oz warm water

3–4 fresh green chillies

cooked basmati rice, to serve

Put the chicken in a non-metallic bowl and rub in the lemon juice and salt. Set aside for 30 minutes.

Meanwhile, purée the garlic, ginger, onion and red chillies in a food processor or blender. Add a little water, if necessary, to help blade movement in a blender.

Heat the oil in a wide shallow pan, preferably non-stick, over a medium–high heat. When the oil is hot, cook the chicken in two batches, until golden brown on all sides. Drain on kitchen paper.

Add the fresh spice paste to the pan with the turmeric and chilli powder and reduce the heat to medium. Cook for 5–6 minutes, stirring regularly.

Add the chicken and warm water. Bring to the boil, reduce the heat to low, cover and cook for 20 minutes. Increase the heat to medium, cover and cook for a further 8–10 minutes, stirring halfway through to ensure that the thickened sauce does not stick to the base of the pan.

Remove the lid and cook until the sauce is reduced to a paste-like consistency, stirring regularly to prevent the sauce from sticking. Add the green chillies, cook for 2–3 mintues, remove from the heat and serve with cooked basmati rice.

Sri Lankan Chicken Curry

The cuisine of Sri Lanka is not dissimilar to that of southern India, whose key ingredients are coconut milk and tamarind. Sri Lankan cuisine is differentiated from this as it uses its own unique blend of curry powder from spices that are dark roasted and ground to a fine powder. This is a delectable curry with a generous amount of chillies, but the pungency is mellowed by rich coconut milk.

SERVES 4

700 g/1 lb 9 oz skinless, boneless
   chicken thighs or breasts

1 tsp salt, or to taste

2 tbsp white wine vinegar

2 tsp coriander seeds

1 tsp cumin seeds

2.5-cm/1-inch piece cinnamon stick,
   broken up

4 cloves

4 green cardamom pods

6 fenugreek seeds

4 dried red chillies, torn into pieces

10–12 curry leaves

4 tbsp sunflower or olive oil

1 large onion, finely chopped

2 tsp ginger purée

2 tsp garlic purée

1 tsp ground turmeric

½ tsp chilli powder

1 lemon grass stalk, finely sliced

200 g/7 oz canned chopped tomatoes

150 ml/5 fl oz warm water

55 g/2 oz creamed coconut, cut into
   small pieces

cooked basmati rice, to serve

Cut the chicken into 5-cm/2-inch chunks and put them in a mixing bowl. Add the salt and vinegar, mix well and set aside for 30 minutes.

Preheat a small heavy-based pan over a medium heat and dry-roast the coriander seeds, cumin seeds, cinnamon, cloves, cardamom, fenugreek, chillies and curry leaves until they are dark, but not black. Remove and cool, then grind in a coffee grinder until finely ground. Set aside.

Heat the oil in a medium saucepan and cook the onion over a medium heat for 5 minutes, until translucent. Add the ginger and garlic purées and continue to cook for a further 2 mintues.

Add the turmeric, chilli powder, chicken and the ground spice mix. Stir and mix well, then add the lemon grass, tomatoes and warm water. Bring to the boil, reduce the heat to low, cover the pan and cook for 25 minutes.

Add the coconut and stir until it has dissolved. Cook for 7–8 minutes, remove from the heat and serve with cooked basmati rice.

Meat

Lamb Pasanda

Here is a legacy from the glorious days of the Mogul courts, when Indian cooking reached a refined peak. The word pasanda, *from which this creamy dish gets its name, indicates small pieces of boneless meat, in this case tender lamb, flattened as thin as possible.*

SERVES 4-6

600 g/1 lb 5 oz boneless shoulder or leg of lamb

2 tbsp garlic and ginger paste

55 g/2 oz ghee or 4 tbsp vegetable or groundnut oil

3 large onions, chopped

1 fresh green chilli, deseeded and chopped

2 green cardamom pods, bruised

1 cinnamon stick, broken in half

2 tsp ground coriander

1 tsp ground cumin

1 tsp ground turmeric

250 ml/9 fl oz water

150 ml/5 fl oz double cream

4 tbsp ground almonds

1½ tsp salt

1 tsp garam masala

paprika and toasted flaked almonds, to garnish

Cut the meat into thin slices, then place the slices between clingfilm and pound with a rolling pin or meat mallet to make them even thinner. Put the lamb slices in a bowl, add the garlic and ginger paste and use your hands to rub the paste into the lamb. Cover and set aside in a cool place to marinate for 2 hours.

Melt the ghee in a large frying pan with a tight-fitting lid over a medium–high heat. Add the onions and chilli and cook, stirring frequently, for 5–8 minutes, until the onions are golden brown.

Stir in the cardamom pods, cinnamon stick, coriander, cumin and turmeric and continue stirring for 2 minutes, or until the spices are aromatic.

Add the meat to the pan and cook, stirring occasionally, for about 5 minutes, until it is brown on all sides and the fat begins to separate. Stir in the water and bring to the boil, still stirring. Reduce the heat to its lowest setting, cover the pan tightly and simmer for 40 minutes, or until the meat is tender.

When the lamb is tender, stir the cream and ground almonds together in a bowl. Beat in 6 tablespoons of the hot cooking liquid from the pan, then gradually beat this mixture back into the pan. Stir in the salt and garam masala. Continue to simmer for a further 5 minutes, uncovered, stirring occasionally.

Garnish with a sprinkling of paprika and toasted flaked almonds and serve.

COOK'S TIP

To toast flaked almonds, put them in a dry frying pan over a medium heat and stir constantly until golden brown. Immediately tip them out of the pan because they can burn quickly.

Lamb in Fragrant Spinach Sauce

This robust home-style dish hails from the northern state of the Punjab, where people love good food drenched in home-made butter! Known as saag gosht, *this dish is traditionally eaten with Indian bread, such as naan or paratha, but it tastes equally good with rice.*

SERVES 4

700 g/1 lb 9 oz boneless leg of lamb

85 g/3 oz whole milk natural yogurt, strained, or Greek-style yogurt

2 tbsp light malt vinegar

2 tsp gram flour

1 tsp ground turmeric

4 tbsp sunflower or olive oil

5-cm/2-inch piece cinnamon stick, halved

5 cloves

5 green cardamom pods, bruised

2 bay leaves

1 large onion, finely chopped

2 tsp garlic purée

2 tsp ginger purée

2 tsp ground cumin

½–1 tsp chilli powder

200 g/7 oz canned chopped tomatoes

175 ml/6 fl oz warm water, plus 4 tbsp

1 tsp salt, or to taste

1 tsp sugar

250 g/9 oz spinach leaves, thawed if frozen, chopped

2 tsp ghee or unsalted butter

1 large garlic clove, finely chopped

¼ tsp freshly grated nutmeg

1 tsp garam masala

125 ml/4 fl oz single cream

Indian bread, to serve

Trim the excess fat from the meat and cut into 2.5-cm/1-inch cubes. Put the yogurt in a non-metallic bowl and beat with a fork or wire whisk until smooth. Add the vinegar, gram flour and turmeric and beat again until well blended. Add the meat and mix thoroughly. Cover and leave to marinate in the refrigerator for 4–5 hours, or overnight. Return to room temperature before cooking.

Heat the oil in a medium heavy-based saucepan over a low heat. Add the cinnamon, cloves, cardamom pods and bay leaves and cook gently, stirring, for 25–30 seconds, then add the onion. Increase the heat to medium and cook, stirring frequently, for 4–5 minutes, until the onion is soft and translucent. Add the garlic and ginger purées and cook for a further 5–6 minutes, until the onion is a pale golden colour.

Add the cumin and chilli powder and cook, stirring, for 1 minute. Add the tomatoes and cook for 5–6 minutes, stirring frequently, then add the 4 tablespoons of warm water. Cook for a further 3 minutes, or until the oil separates from the spice paste. Add the marinated meat, increase the heat slightly and cook, stirring, for 5–6 minutes, until the meat changes colour. Add the salt and sugar, stir, then pour in the 175 ml/6 fl oz warm water. Bring to the boil, then reduce the heat to low, cover and simmer, stirring occasionally, for 55–60 minutes.

Meanwhile, blanch the spinach in a large saucepan of boiling water for 2 minutes. Drain and immediately plunge into cold water. Melt the ghee in a separate medium saucepan over a low heat. Add the chopped garlic and cook, stirring, until the garlic is light brown. Stir in the nutmeg and garam masala. Squeeze out the excess water from the spinach, add to the spiced butter and stir to mix thoroughly. Add the spinach mixture to the curry, then add the cream. Stir to mix well and simmer, uncovered, for 2–3 minutes. Remove from the heat and serve immediately with Indian bread.

Lamb Rogan Josh

Originally from Kashmir, this fragrant rich dish was quickly adopted by Mogul cooks and has remained a firm favourite in northern India ever since. A Kashmiri natural dye called rattanjog *originally provided the characteristic red colour, but chilli powder and tomato purée provide a more readily available, and less expensive, alternative in this recipe.*

SERVES 4

350 ml/12 fl oz natural yogurt

½ tsp ground asafoetida, dissolved in 2 tbsp water

700 g/1 lb 9 oz boneless leg of lamb, trimmed and cut into 5-cm/2-inch cubes

2 tomatoes, deseeded and chopped

1 onion, chopped

25 g/1 oz ghee or 2 tbsp vegetable or groundnut oil

1½ tbsp garlic and ginger paste

2 tbsp tomato purée

2 bay leaves

1 tbsp ground coriander

¼–1 tsp chilli powder, ideally Kashmiri chilli powder

½ tsp ground turmeric

1 tsp salt

½ tsp garam masala

Put the yogurt in a large bowl and stir in the dissolved asafoetida. Add the lamb and use your hands to rub in all the marinade, then set aside for 30 minutes.

Meanwhile, put the tomatoes and onion in a blender and process until blended.

Melt the ghee in a flameproof casserole or large frying pan with a tight-fitting lid. Add the garlic and ginger paste and stir around until the aromas are released. Stir in the tomato mixture, tomato purée, bay leaves, coriander, chilli powder and turmeric, reduce the heat to low and simmer, stirring occasionally, for 5–8 minutes.

Add the lamb and salt with any leftover marinade and stir around for 2 minutes. Cover, reduce the heat to low and simmer, stirring occasionally, for 30 minutes. The lamb should give off enough moisture to prevent it from catching on the base of the pan, but if the sauce looks too dry, stir in a little water.

Sprinkle with the garam masala, re-cover the pan and continue simmering for 15–20 minutes, until the lamb is tender. Serve immediately.

COOK'S TIP

For an authentic flavour, search out the bright red Kashmiri chilli powder sold in Indian stores.

Lamb Dhansak

For India's numerous Parsis, this rich dish is served for a Sunday family lunch. The lentils and pumpkin dissolve into a velvety smooth sauce, and all that are needed to complete the meal are rice and naans.

SERVES 4-6

700 g/1 lb 9 oz boneless shoulder of
    lamb, trimmed and cut into 5-cm/
    2-inch cubes

1 tbsp garlic and ginger paste

5 green cardamom pods

200 g/7 oz yellow lentils (toor dal)

100 g/3½ oz pumpkin, peeled, deseeded
    and chopped

1 carrot, thinly sliced

1 fresh green chilli, deseeded and
    chopped

1 tsp fenugreek powder

500 ml/18 fl oz water

1 large onion, thinly sliced

30 g/1 oz ghee or 2 tbsp vegetable or
    groundnut oil

2 garlic cloves, crushed

salt

chopped fresh coriander,
    to garnish

DHANSAK MASALA

1 tsp garam masala

½ tsp ground coriander

½ tsp ground cumin

½ tsp chilli powder

½ tsp ground turmeric

¼ tsp ground cardamom

¼ tsp ground cloves

Put the lamb and 1 teaspoon of salt in a large saucepan with enough water to cover and bring to the boil. Reduce the heat and simmer, skimming the surface as necessary until no more foam rises. Stir in the garlic and ginger paste and cardamom pods and continue simmering for a total of 30 minutes.

Meanwhile, put the lentils, pumpkin, carrot, chilli and fenugreek powder in a large heavy-based saucepan and pour over the water. Bring to the boil, stirring occasionally, then reduce the heat and simmer for 20–30 minutes, until the lentils and carrot are very tender. Stir in a little extra water if the lentils look as though they will catch on the base of the pan.

Leave the lentil mixture to cool slightly, then pour it into a food processor or blender and whizz until a thick, smooth sauce forms.

While the lamb and lentils are cooking, put the onion in a bowl, sprinkle with 1 teaspoon of salt and leave to stand for about 5 minutes to extract the moisture. Use your hands to squeeze out the moisture.

Melt the ghee in a flameproof casserole or large frying pan with a tight-fitting lid over a high heat. Add the onion and cook, stirring constantly, for 2 minutes. Remove one third of the onion and continue frying the rest for a further 1–2 minutes, until golden brown. Use a slotted spoon to immediately remove the onion from the pan, as it will continue to darken as it cools.

Return the one third of the onion to the pan with the garlic. Stir in all the dhansak masala ingredients and cook for 2 minutes, stirring constantly. Add the cooked lamb and stir for a further 2 minutes. Add the lentil sauce and simmer over a medium heat to warm through, stirring and adding a little extra water, if needed. Adjust the seasoning, if necessary. Sprinkle with the remaining onion and serve, garnished with coriander.

Lamb Shanks Marathani

From Mumbai, this dish is bursting with lots of flavours that reflect the city's vibrancy and diversity. It's not for nothing that the port city is known as 'The Gateway to India', as traders from all corners of the globe have always sold their wares here. Marathani in a recipe title indicates that a dish comes from the state of Maharashtra, of which Mumbai is the capital.

SERVES 4

55 g/2 oz ghee or 4 tbsp vegetable
  or groundnut oil

2 large onions, thinly sliced

40 g/1½ oz cashew nuts

1½ tbsp garlic and ginger paste

2 fresh green chillies, deseeded and
  chopped

2 cinnamon sticks, broken in half

½ tsp chilli powder

½ tsp ground turmeric

½ tsp ground coriander

¼ tsp ground mace

3 tbsp natural yogurt

4 lamb shanks

850 ml/1½ pints water

½ tsp garam masala

salt and pepper

chopped fresh coriander, to garnish

cooked basmati rice, to serve

Melt half the ghee in a large flameproof casserole over a medium–high heat. Add the onions and cook, stirring frequently, for 5–8 minutes, until soft but not coloured. Stir in the cashew nuts and stir around for just 1–2 minutes, until they turn light brown.

Use a slotted spoon to remove the onions and nuts from the casserole and leave to cool slightly. Transfer both to a food processor or mortar and grind to a paste.

Melt the remaining ghee in the casserole. Add the garlic and ginger paste, chillies and cinnamon and stir around for about 1 minute, until you can smell the aromas.

Stir in the chilli powder, turmeric, coriander and mace. Gradually stir in the yogurt, stirring constantly. Add the lamb shanks and continue stirring for about 5 minutes, until the yogurt is absorbed.

Stir in the reserved onion and cashew paste. Pour in enough of the water to cover the lamb shanks, add the garam masala and bring to the boil. Reduce the heat to low, cover the casserole and leave to simmer for 1¾–2 hours, until the lamb is very tender and almost falling off the bones.

Taste and adjust the seasoning, if necessary. Transfer the lamb shanks to a serving dish and spoon over the thin sauce. Garnish with chopped coriander and serve with cooked basmati rice.

Lamb in Cinnamon-scented Fenugreek Sauce

This lovely north Indian dish bursts with flavours of powerful fenugreek, pungent chillies, aromatic cloves and sweet cinnamon. The lamb is marinated in red wine vinegar, ginger and garlic, and gentle, prolonged cooking enables the meat to absorb all the wonderful flavours.

SERVES 4

700 g/1 lb 9 oz boneless leg or neck end
   of lamb, cut into 2.5-cm/1-inch cubes

4 tbsp red wine vinegar

1 tsp salt, or to taste

4 tbsp sunflower or olive oil

5-cm/2-inch piece cinnamon stick,
   halved

5 green cardamom pods, bruised

5 cloves

1 large onion, finely chopped

2 tsp ginger purée

2 tsp garlic purée

2 tsp ground cumin

1 tsp ground turmeric

½–1 tsp chilli powder

225 g/8 oz canned chopped tomatoes

1½ tbsp dried fenugreek leaves

175 ml/6 fl oz warm water

2 tsp ghee or unsalted butter

½ tsp garam masala

fresh coriander sprigs, to garnish

Indian bread or cooked basmati rice,
   to serve

Put the meat in a non-metallic bowl and rub in the vinegar and salt. Set aside for 30–40 minutes.

Heat the oil in a medium heavy-based saucepan over a low heat and add the cinnamon, cardamom and cloves. Let them sizzle for 25–30 seconds, then add the onion, increase the heat to medium and cook, stirring regularly, until the onion is soft but not brown.

Add the ginger and garlic purées and cook for a further 2–3 minutes, then add the cumin, turmeric and chilli powder. Cook for 1–2 minutes and add the tomatoes. Increase the heat slightly and continue to cook until the tomatoes are reduced to a paste-like consistency and the oil separates from the paste. Reduce the heat towards the last 2–3 minutes.

Add the meat, fenugreek leaves and warm water. Bring to the boil, reduce the heat to low, cover and simmer for 45–50 minutes, or until the meat is tender.

In a small pan, melt the ghee over a low heat and stir in the garam masala. Cook for 30 seconds, then fold this spiced mixture into the curry. Remove from the heat, garnish with coriander sprigs and serve with Indian bread or cooked basmati rice.

Peshawar-style Lamb Curry

Peshawar, in the North West Frontier Province, was created during the British Raj to safeguard India from foreign invaders. The cuisine of this area is famous for its robust flavours and brilliant colours. This lamb curry is in a class of its own.

SERVES 4

4 tbsp sunflower or olive oil

2.5-cm/1-inch piece cinnamon stick

5 green cardamom pods, bruised

5 cloves

2 bay leaves

700 g/1 lb 9 oz boneless leg of lamb, cut into 2.5-cm/1-inch cubes

1 large onion, finely chopped

2 tsp ginger purée

2 tsp garlic purée

1 tbsp tomato purée

1 tsp ground turmeric

1 tsp ground coriander

1 tsp ground cumin

125 g/4½ oz thick set natural yogurt

2 tsp gram flour or corn flour

½-1 tsp chilli powder

150 ml/5 fl oz warm water

1 tbsp chopped fresh mint leaves

2 tbsp chopped fresh coriander leaves

Indian bread, to serve

In a medium saucepan, heat the oil over a low heat and add the cinnamon, cardamom, cloves and bay leaves. Let them sizzle for 25–30 seconds, then add the meat, increase the heat to medium–high and cook until the meat begins to brown and all the natural juices have evaporated.

Add the onion and ginger and garlic purées, cook for 5–6 minutes, stirring regularly, then add the tomato purée, turmeric, ground coriander and cumin. Continue to cook for 3–4 minutes.

Whisk together the yogurt, gram flour and chilli powder and add to the meat. Reduce the heat to low, add the warm water, cover and simmer, stirring to ensure that the sauce does not stick to the base of the pan, for 45–50 minutes, or until the meat is tender. Simmer uncovered, if necessary, to thicken the sauce to a desired consistency.

Stir in the fresh mint and coriander, remove from the heat and serve with Indian bread.

Kheema Matar

When the cold winter winds come to northern India, this simple, rustic dish makes a popular family meal.

SERVES 4-6

30 g/1 oz ghee or 2 tbsp vegetable
  or groundnut oil

2 tsp cumin seeds

1 large onion, finely chopped

1 tbsp garlic and ginger paste

2 bay leaves

1 tsp mild, medium or hot curry powder,
  to taste

2 tomatoes, deseeded and chopped

1 tsp ground coriander

¼–½ tsp chilli powder

¼ tsp ground turmeric

pinch of sugar

½ teaspoon salt

½ teaspoon pepper

500 g/1 lb 2 oz lean minced beef
  or lamb

250 g/9 oz frozen peas, straight from
  the freezer

Melt the ghee in a flameproof casserole or large frying pan with a tight-fitting lid. Add the cumin seeds and cook, stirring, for 30 seconds, or until they start to crackle.

Stir in the onion, garlic and ginger paste, bay leaves and curry powder and continue to stir-fry until the fat separates.

Stir in the tomatoes and cook for 1–2 minutes. Stir in the coriander, chilli powder, turmeric, sugar, salt and pepper and stir around for 30 seconds.

Add the beef and cook for 5 minutes, using a wooden spoon to break up the meat, or until it is no longer pink. Reduce the heat and simmer, stirring occasionally, for 10 minutes.

Add the peas and continue simmering for a further 10–15 minutes, until the peas are thawed and hot. If there is too much liquid left in the pan, increase the heat and let it bubble for a few minutes until it reduces.

Beef Madras

This spicy curry with a hint of coconut gets its Indian name from the south-eastern coastal town of Chennai, formerly known as Madras. The regional specialities are typically flavoured with coconut and lots of chillies, which is why restaurant menus frequently label every hot dish as 'madras'.

SERVES 4-6

1–2 dried red chillies

2 tsp ground coriander

2 tsp ground turmeric

1 tsp black mustard seeds

½ tsp ground ginger

¼ tsp pepper

140 g/5 oz creamed coconut, grated, dissolved in 300 ml/10 fl oz boiling water

55 g/2 oz ghee or 4 tbsp vegetable or groundnut oil

2 onions, chopped

3 large garlic cloves, chopped

700 g/1 lb 9 oz lean stewing steak, such as chuck, trimmed and cut into 5-cm/2-inch cubes

250 ml/9 fl oz beef stock

lemon juice

salt

Depending on how hot you want this dish to be, chop the chillies with or without any seeds. The more seeds you include, the hotter the dish will be. Put the chopped chilli and any seeds in a small bowl with the coriander, turmeric, mustard seeds, ginger and pepper and stir in a little of the dissolved creamed coconut to make a thin paste.

Melt the ghee in a flameproof casserole or large frying pan with a tight-fitting lid over a medium–high heat. Add the onions and garlic and cook for 5–8 minutes, stirring frequently, until the onion is golden brown. Add the spice paste and stir around for 2 minutes, or until you can smell the aromas.

Add the meat and stock and bring to the boil. Reduce the heat to its lowest level, cover tightly and simmer for 1½ hours, or until the beef is tender. Check occasionally that the meat isn't catching on the base of the pan and stir in a little extra water or stock, if necessary.

Uncover the pan and stir in the remaining dissolved coconut cream with the lemon juice and salt to taste. Bring to the boil, stirring, then reduce the heat again and simmer, still uncovered, until the sauce reduces slightly.

COOK'S TIP
The dish takes on a different character, but is equally flavoursome, if you omit the chillies altogether and garnish with toasted coconut flakes just before serving.

Balti Beef

Direct from Birmingham, England, this is the Indian/Pakistani version of stir-frying. Immigrants introduced Brummies to this quick style of cooking and now balti restaurants thrive throughout the UK and Europe. It's quick cooking once you've made the balti sauce, but that can be made in advance and refrigerated for several days.

SERVES 4-6

30 g/1 oz ghee or 2 tbsp vegetable or
  groundnut oil

1 large onion, chopped

2 garlic cloves, crushed

2 large red peppers, deseeded and
  chopped

600 g/1 lb 5 oz boneless beef, such as
  sirloin, thinly sliced

fresh coriander sprigs, to garnish

Indian bread, to serve

BALTI SAUCE

30 g/1 oz ghee or 2 tbsp vegetable or
  groundnut oil

2 large onions, chopped

1 tbsp garlic and ginger paste

400 g/14 oz canned chopped tomatoes

1 tsp ground paprika

½ tsp ground turmeric

½ tsp ground cumin

½ tsp ground coriander

¼ tsp chilli powder

¼ tsp ground cardamom

1 bay leaf

salt and pepper

To make the balti sauce, melt the ghee in a wok or large frying pan over a medium–high heat. Add the onions and garlic and ginger paste and stir-fry for about 5 minutes, until the onion is golden brown. Stir in the tomatoes, then add the paprika, turmeric, cumin, coriander, chilli powder, cardamom, bay leaf and salt and pepper to taste. Bring to the boil, stirring, then reduce the heat and simmer for 20 minutes, stirring occasionally.

Leave the sauce to cool slightly, then remove the bay leaf and pour the mixture into a food processor or blender and whizz to a smooth sauce.

Wipe out the wok and return it to a medium–high heat. Add the ghee and melt. Add the onion and garlic and stir-fry for 5–8 minutes, until golden brown. Add the red peppers and continue stir-frying for 2 minutes.

Stir in the beef and continue stirring for 2 minutes, until it starts to turn brown. Add the balti sauce and bring to the boil. Reduce the heat and simmer for 5 minutes, or until the sauce slightly reduces again and the pepper is tender. Adjust the seasoning, if necessary. Garnish with coriander sprigs and serve with Indian bread.

Coconut Beef Curry

This rich and aromatic curry uses Mussaman curry paste, which is a Thai curry paste with Islamic origins. It is unusual because it contains a number of spices that are more common in Indian cuisine than in Thai, such as cloves, cardamom, coriander and cumin.

SERVES 4

1 tbsp ground coriander

1 tbsp ground cumin

3 tbsp Mussaman curry paste

150 ml/5 fl oz water

75 g/2¾ oz creamed coconut

450 g/1 lb beef fillet, cut into strips

400 ml/14 fl oz coconut milk

50 g/1¾ oz unsalted peanuts, finely chopped

2 tbsp fish sauce

1 tsp palm sugar or soft light brown sugar

4 kaffir lime leaves

fresh coriander sprigs, to garnish

cooked rice, to serve

Combine the coriander, cumin and curry paste in a bowl. Pour the water into a saucepan, add the creamed coconut and heat until it has dissolved. Add the curry paste mixture and simmer for 1 minute.

Add the beef and simmer for 6–8 minutes, then add the coconut milk, peanuts, fish sauce and sugar. Simmer gently for 15–20 minutes, until the meat is tender.

Add the lime leaves and simmer for 1–2 minutes. Garnish with coriander sprigs and serve with cooked rice.

Beef Rendang

Prime-quality beef is essential to make a good rendang. *Although other meats, such as chicken, lamb and pork, are also used, beef is by far the best choice in a traditional* rendang, *which is enjoyed all over Indonesia with plain boiled rice. The quantity of chillies may seem excessive, but the pungency is mellowed by the two different ways in which the coconut is used.*

SERVES 4

5–6 dried red chillies

2–3 fresh red chillies, roughly chopped

4–5 shallots or 1 large onion, roughly chopped

4 large garlic cloves, roughly chopped

2.5-cm/1-inch piece fresh ginger, roughly chopped

2 tbsp water

1 tsp coriander seeds

1 tsp cumin seeds

55 g/2 oz desiccated coconut

4 tbsp groundnut oil

700 g/1 lb 9 oz prime-quality casserole beef, fat trimmed and cut into 2.5-cm/1-inch cubes

1 tbsp dark soy sauce

1 lemon grass stalk, finely chopped

3 kaffir lime leaves, shredded, plus extra to garnish

½ tsp salt

200 ml/7 fl oz warm water

1 tbsp tamarind juice

400 ml/14 fl oz coconut milk

toasted flaked coconut, to garnish

cooked rice, to serve

Soak the dried chillies in boiling water for 10 minutes, then drain and place in a food processor or blender. Add the fresh chillies, shallots, garlic, ginger and the 2 tablespoons of water, and blend until the ingredients are smooth.

Preheat a small heavy-based pan over a medium heat and add the coriander and cumin seeds. Stir for about a minute, until they release their aroma, then remove them from the pan and let cool. In the same pan, dry-roast the desiccated coconut, stirring constantly, until it is tinged with a light brown colour. Remove from the pan and cool, then mix the coconut with the roasted spices, and grind them in two batches in a coffee grinder.

Heat the oil in a medium saucepan and add the puréed ingredients. Cook over a medium heat, stirring regularly, for 5–6 minutes. Add a little water to prevent the mixture from sticking and continue to cook for a further 5–6 minutes, adding water if necessary.

Add the meat and increase the heat to medium–high, stir until the meat changes colour, and add the roasted coconut mixture, soy sauce, lemon grass, lime leaves and salt. Stir and mix well and pour in the warm water. Bring to the boil, reduce the heat to low, cover and simmer for 45 minutes, stirring occasionally to ensure that the mixture does not stick to the bottom of the pan.

Add the tamarind juice and coconut milk, bring to a gentle simmer, cover and cook for a further 45 minutes, or until the meat is tender. Remove the lid and cook over a medium heat, if necessary, to thicken the sauce. Garnish with the toasted coconut and shredded lime leaves and serve with cooked rice.

Mussaman Curry

A very traditional dish that combines potatoes and peanuts with tender beef fillet, and tastes fantastic!

SERVES 4

2 tbsp groundnut or vegetable oil

225 g/8 oz shallots, roughly chopped

1 garlic clove, crushed

450 g/1 lb beef fillet, thickly
  sliced and then cut into 2.5-cm/
  1-inch cubes

2 tbsp Mussaman curry paste

3 potatoes, cut into 2.5-cm/1-inch cubes

400 ml/14 fl oz coconut milk

2 tbsp soy sauce

150 ml/5 fl oz beef stock

1 tsp palm sugar or soft light brown
  sugar

85 g/3 oz unsalted peanuts

handful of fresh coriander, chopped

cooked rice or noodles, to serve

Heat the oil in a preheated wok, add the shallots and garlic and stir-fry over a medium–high heat for 1–2 minutes, until softened. Add the beef and curry paste and stir-fry over a high heat for 2–3 minutes, until browned all over. Add the potatoes, coconut milk, soy sauce, stock and sugar and bring gently to the boil, stirring occasionally. Reduce the heat and simmer for 8–10 minutes, until the potatoes are tender.

Meanwhile, heat a separate dry frying pan until hot, add the peanuts and cook over a medium–high heat, shaking the frying pan frequently, for 2–3 minutes, until lightly browned. Add to the curry with the coriander and stir well. Serve hot with rice or noodles.

COOK'S TIP

To help the skins of the shallots come off more easily, put them in a heatproof bowl, cover with boiling water and leave for 10 minutes.

Pork Vindaloo

The name vindaloo *is derived from two Portuguese words:* vin, *meaning 'vinegar', and* alho, *meaning 'garlic'. When the Portuguese travelled to India, they took pork preserved in vinegar, garlic and pepper, which was spiced up to suit Indian tastes!*

SERVES 4

2–6 dried red chillies (long slim variety), torn into 2–3 pieces

5 cloves

2.5-cm/1-inch piece cinnamon stick, broken up

4 green cardamom pods

½ tsp black peppercorns

½ mace blade

¼ nutmeg, lightly crushed

1 tsp cumin seeds

1½ tsp coriander seeds

½ tsp fenugreek seeds

2 tsp garlic purée

1 tbsp ginger purée

3 tbsp cider vinegar or white wine vinegar

1 tbsp tamarind juice or juice of ½ lime

700 g/1 lb 9 oz boneless leg of pork, cut into 2.5-cm/1-inch cubes

4 tbsp sunflower or olive oil, plus 2 tsp

2 large onions, finely chopped

250 ml/9 fl oz warm water, plus 4 tbsp

1 tsp salt, or to taste

1 tsp soft dark brown sugar

2 large garlic cloves, finely sliced

8–10 fresh or dried curry leaves

cooked basmati rice, to serve

Grind the first 10 ingredients (all the spices) to a fine powder in a coffee grinder. Transfer the ground spices to a bowl and add the garlic and ginger purées, vinegar and tamarind juice. Mix together to form a paste.

Put the pork in a large non-metallic bowl and rub about one quarter of the spice paste into the meat. Cover and leave to marinate in the refrigerator for 30–40 minutes.

Heat the 4 tablespoons of oil in a medium heavy-based saucepan over a medium heat, add the onions and cook, stirring frequently, for 8–10 minutes, until lightly browned. Add the remaining spice paste and cook, stirring constantly, for 5–6 minutes. Add 2 tablespoons of the warm water and cook until it evaporates. Repeat with another 2 tablespoons of water.

Add the marinated pork and cook over medium–high heat for 5–6 minutes, until the meat changes colour. Add the salt, sugar and the remaining 250 ml/9 fl oz warm water. Bring to the boil, then reduce the heat to low, cover and simmer for 50–55 minutes, until the meat is tender.

Meanwhile, heat the 2 teaspoons of oil in a very small saucepan over a low heat. Add the sliced garlic and cook, stirring frequently, until it begins to brown. Add the curry leaves and leave to sizzle for 15–20 seconds. Stir the garlic mixture into the vindaloo. Remove from the heat and serve immediately with cooked basmati rice.

Railway Pork & Vegetables

East meets West in the Christian Anglo-Indian kitchens of Kolkata, where the tradition of flavouring British-style dishes with Indian ingredients lives on. This example, not unlike a British savoury pie filling, is an updated version of the railway curries once served in dining cars.

SERVES 4-6

40 g/1½ oz ghee or 3 tbsp vegetable or
   groundnut oil

1 large onion, finely chopped

4 green cardamom pods

3 cloves

1 cinnamon stick

1 tbsp garlic and ginger paste

2 tsp garam masala

¼–½ tsp chilli powder

½ tsp ground asafoetida

2 tsp salt

600 g/1 lb 5 oz lean minced pork

1 potato, scrubbed and cut into 5 mm/
   ¼-inch dice

400 g/14 oz canned chopped tomatoes

125 ml/4 fl oz water

1 bay leaf

1 large carrot, coarsely grated

Melt the ghee in a flameproof casserole or large frying pan with a tight-fitting lid over a medium heat. Add the onion and cook, stirring occasionally, for 5–8 minutes, until golden brown. Add the cardamom pods, cloves and cinnamon stick and cook, stirring, for 1 minute, or until you can smell the aromas.

Add the garlic and ginger paste, garam masala, chilli powder, asafoetida and salt and stir around for a further minute. Add the pork and cook for 5 minutes, or until no longer pink, using a wooden spoon to break up the meat.

Add the potato, tomatoes, water and bay leaf and bring to the boil, stirring. Reduce the heat to the lowest level, cover tightly and simmer for 15 minutes. Stir in the carrot and simmer for a further 5 minutes, or until the potato and carrot are tender. Taste and adjust the seasoning, if necessary, and serve.

COOK'S TIP
Lean minced lamb or beef can be used instead of the pork.

Red Curry Pork with Peppers

This dish of is a delightful combination of succulent pork, tender mushrooms and sweet red peppers. The mushrooms act like little sponges, soaking up the fragrant coconut sauce beautifully.

SERVES 4

2 tbsp vegetable or groundnut oil

1 onion, roughly chopped

2 garlic cloves, chopped

450 g/1 lb pork fillet, thickly sliced

1 red pepper, deseeded and cut into
   squares

175 g/6 oz mushrooms, quartered

2 tbsp Thai red curry paste

115 g/4 oz creamed coconut, chopped

300 ml/10 fl oz pork or vegetable stock

2 tbsp Thai soy sauce

4 tomatoes, peeled, deseeded and
   chopped

handful of fresh coriander, chopped,
   plus extra to garnish

cooked rice noodles, to serve

Heat the oil in a wok or large frying pan and cook the onion and garlic for 1–2 minutes, until they are soft but not brown.

Add the pork slices and stir-fry for 2–3 minutes, until brown all over. Add the red pepper, mushrooms and curry paste.

Dissolve the creamed coconut in the stock and add to the wok with the soy sauce. Bring to the boil and simmer for 4–5 minutes, until the liquid has reduced and thickened.

Add the tomatoes and coriander and cook for 1–2 minutes. Garnish with extra chopped coriander and serve with cooked rice noodles.

Pork with Mixed Green Beans

Quick and convenient, this tasty Thai-style pork curry uses a mixture of different beans – French beans, broad beans and runner beans – and envelopes them in a spicy sauce enriched with peanuts.

SERVES 4

2 tbsp vegetable or groundnut oil

2 shallots, chopped

225 g/8 oz pork fillet, thinly sliced

2.5-cm/1-inch piece fresh galangal, thinly sliced

2 garlic cloves, chopped

300 ml/10 fl oz chicken stock

4 tbsp chilli sauce

4 tbsp crunchy peanut butter

115 g/4 oz fine French beans, trimmed

115 g/4 oz frozen broad beans

115 g/4 oz runner beans, trimmed and sliced

crispy noodles, to serve

Heat the oil in a wok and stir-fry the shallots, pork, galangal and garlic until lightly browned.

Add the stock, chilli sauce and peanut butter and stir until the peanut butter has melted. Add all the beans and simmer for 3–4 minutes. Serve hot with crispy noodles.

Pork with Cinnamon & Fenugreek

This is a dry dish, that is, one served without an integral sauce. Fenugreek is an aromatic, pungent herb and both the leaves and seeds are used in Asian cooking. It is a common ingredient in curry powders but should be used sparingly because it can be overpowering.

SERVES 4

1 tsp ground coriander

1 tsp ground cumin

1 tsp chilli powder

1 tbsp dried fenugreek leaves

1 tsp ground fenugreek

150 ml/5 fl oz natural yogurt

450 g/1 lb diced pork fillet

4 tbsp ghee or vegetable oil

1 large onion, sliced

5-cm/2-inch piece fresh ginger, finely chopped

4 garlic cloves, finely chopped

1 cinnamon stick

6 green cardamom pods

6 whole cloves

2 bay leaves

175 ml/6 fl oz water

salt

Mix the coriander, cumin, chilli powder, dried fenugreek, ground fenugreek and yogurt together in a small bowl. Place the pork in a large, shallow non-metallic dish and add the spice mixture, turning well to coat. Cover with clingfilm and leave to marinate in the refrigerator for 30 minutes.

Melt the ghee in a large heavy-based saucepan. Cook the onion over a low heat, stirring occasionally, for 5 minutes, or until soft. Add the ginger, garlic, cinnamon stick, cardamom pods, cloves and bay leaves and cook, stirring constantly, for 2 minutes, or until the spices give off their aroma. Add the meat with its marinade and the water, and season to taste with salt. Bring to the boil, reduce the heat, cover and simmer for 30 minutes.

Transfer the meat mixture to a preheated wok or large heavy-based frying pan and cook over a low heat, stirring constantly, until dry and tender. If necessary, occasionally sprinkle with a little water to prevent it from sticking to the wok. Serve immediately.

COOK'S TIP
This recipe would also work well with lean lamb or rump steak instead of the pork, if you prefer.

Burmese Pork Curry

The predominant flavour in this curry comes from a very generous quantity of garlic and ginger, which is also a way in which the Burmese preserve their meat. In Burma, vinegar is used for flavouring as well as for preservation. In this recipe, however, dry white wine has been used, which tenderizes the meat beautifully and also acts as a preservative.

SERVES 4

700 g/1 lb 9 oz boned leg of pork, fat trimmed and cut into 2.5-cm/1-inch cubes

2 tbsp dry white wine

1 tsp salt, or to taste

8 large garlic cloves, roughly chopped

5-cm/2-inch piece fresh ginger, roughly chopped

2 fresh red chillies, roughly chopped

1 large onion, roughly chopped

1 tsp ground turmeric

½–1 tsp chilli powder

3 tbsp groundnut oil

1 tbsp sesame oil

200 ml/7 fl oz warm water

1 fresh green chilli, deseeded and cut into julienne strips, to garnish

cooked basmati rice, to serve

Mix the meat, wine and salt in a non-metallic bowl and set aside for 1 hour.

Put the garlic, ginger, chillies and onion in a food processor or blender and blend until the ingredients are mushy. Transfer to a bowl and stir in the turmeric and chilli powder.

Heat both types of oil in a medium heavy-based saucepan over a medium heat, and add the puréed ingredients. Stir and cook for 5–6 minutes, reduce the heat to low and continue to cook for a further 8–10 minutes, sprinkling over a tablespoon of water from time to time to prevent the spices from sticking to the base of the pan.

Add the marinated pork, increase the heat to medium–high and stir until the meat changes colour. Pour in the warm water, bring to the boil, reduce the heat to low, cover and cook for 1 hour 10 minutes, stirring several times during the last 15–20 minutes to prevent the thickened sauce from sticking. Remove from the heat and garnish with the strips of chilli. Serve with cooked basmati rice.

Meatballs in Creamy Cashew Nut Sauce

Known as rista, *this delectable recipe comes from Kashmir, the northernmost state in India, with a rich culinary heritage. Kashmiri cooking is a work of art and the chefs of this beautiful Himalayan state are extremely skilled as well as creative.*

SERVES 4

125 g/4½ oz raw cashew nuts

150 ml/5 fl oz boiling water

450 g/1 lb fresh lean lamb mince

1 tbsp thick set natural yogurt

1 medium egg, beaten

½ tsp ground cardamom

½ tsp ground nutmeg

½ tsp pepper

½ tsp dried mint

½ tsp salt, or to taste

300 ml/10 fl oz water

2.5-cm/1-inch piece cinnamon stick

5 green cardamom pods

5 cloves

2 bay leaves

3 tbsp sunflower or olive oil

1 onion, finely chopped

2 tsp garlic purée

1 tsp ground ginger

1 tsp ground fennel seeds

½ tsp ground turmeric

½–1 tsp chilli powder

150 ml/5 fl oz double cream

1 tbsp crushed pistachio nuts, to garnish

Indian bread or cooked rice, to serve

Soak the cashews in the boiling water for 20 minutes.

Put the lamb mince in a mixing bowl and add the yogurt, egg, cardamom, nutmeg, pepper, mint and salt. Knead the mince until it is smooth and velvety. Alternatively, put the ingredients in a food processor and process until fine. Chill the mixture for 30–40 minutes, then divide it into quarters. Make five balls (koftas) out of each quarter and compress so that they are firm, rolling them between your palms to make them smooth and neat.

Bring the 300 ml/10 fl oz water to the boil in a large shallow pan and add all the whole spices and the bay leaves. Arrange the meatballs in a single layer in the spiced liquid, reduce the heat to medium, cover the pan and cook for 12–15 minutes.

Remove the meatballs, cover and keep hot. Strain the spiced stock and set aside.

Wipe out the pan and add the oil. Place over a medium heat and add the onion and garlic purée. Cook until the mixture begins to brown and add the ground ginger, ground fennel seeds, turmeric and chilli powder. Stir-fry for 2–3 minutes, then add the strained stock and meatballs. Bring to the boil, reduce the heat to low, cover and simmer for 10–12 minutes.

Meanwhile, purée the cashews in a blender and add to the meatball mixture along with the cream. Simmer for a further 5–6 minutes, then remove from the heat. Garnish with crushed pistachio nuts and serve with Indian bread or cooked rice.

Fish & Seafood

Goan Fish Curry

Goa is well known for its fish and shellfish dishes, which are usually cooked in coconut milk. For this dish salmon has been chosen because its firm flesh lends itself well to curry dishes and takes on the flavours of all the spices.

SERVES 4

4 skinless salmon fillets, about 200 g/7 oz each

1 tsp salt, or to taste

1 tbsp lemon juice

3 tbsp sunflower or olive oil

1 large onion, finely chopped

2 tsp garlic purée

2 tsp ginger purée

½ tsp ground turmeric

1 tsp ground coriander

½ tsp ground cumin

½–1 tsp chilli powder

250 ml/9 fl oz coconut milk

2–3 fresh green chillies, sliced lengthways (deseeded if you like)

2 tbsp cider vinegar or white wine vinegar

2 tbsp chopped fresh coriander leaves

cooked basmati rice, to serve

Cut each salmon fillet in half and lay on a plate in a single layer. Sprinkle with half the salt and all of the lemon juice and rub in gently. Cover and leave to marinate in the refrigerator for 15–20 minutes.

Heat the oil in a frying pan over a medium heat, add the onion and cook, stirring frequently to ensure even colouring, for 8–9 minutes, until a pale golden colour.

Add the garlic and ginger purées and cook, stirring, for 1 minute, then add the turmeric, ground coriander, cumin and chilli powder and cook, stirring, for 1 minute. Add the coconut milk, chillies and vinegar, then the remaining salt, stir well and simmer, uncovered, for 6–8 minutes.

Add the fish and cook gently for 5–6 minutes. Stir in the fresh coriander and remove from the heat. Serve immediately with cooked basmati rice.

COOK'S TIP

This curry improves in flavour if you cook it in advance and reheat very gently before serving. You can safely store it in the refrigerator for up to 48 hours.

Thai Fish Curry

The beauty of this curry is in the mouth-watering combination of white fish and oily fish, both of which are extremely beneficial for the health. Make sure you serve this dish with plenty of fragrant jasmine rice to soak up the delicious juices.

SERVES 4

juice of 1 lime

4 tbsp fish sauce

2 tbsp Thai soy sauce

1 fresh red chilli, deseeded and chopped

350 g/12 oz monkfish fillet,
   cut into cubes

350 g/12 oz salmon fillets, skinned and
   cut into cubes

400 ml/14 fl oz coconut milk

3 kaffir lime leaves

1 tbsp Thai red curry paste

1 lemon grass stalk (white part only),
   finely chopped

cooked jasmine rice with chopped fresh
   coriander, to serve

Combine the lime juice, half the fish sauce and all of the soy sauce in a shallow non-metallic dish. Add the chilli and the fish, stir to coat, cover with clingfilm and chill for 1–2 hours, or overnight.

Bring the coconut milk to the boil in a saucepan and add the lime leaves, curry paste, the remaining fish sauce and the lemon grass. Simmer gently for 10–15 minutes.

Add the fish with its marinade and simmer gently for 4–5 minutes, until the fish is cooked. Serve hot accompanied by cooked jasmine rice with chopped coriander stirred through it.

Balti Fish Curry

This is for those who prefer robustly flavoured dishes, more like the ones served in northern India than the coconut-based ones from the south.

SERVES 4-6

900 g/2 lb thick fish fillets, such as
monkfish, grey mullet, cod or
haddock, rinsed and cut into large
chunks

2 bay leaves, torn

140 g/5 oz ghee or 150 ml/5 fl oz
vegetable or groundnut oil

2 large onions, chopped

½ tbsp salt

150 ml/5 fl oz water

chopped fresh coriander, to garnish

Indian bread, to serve

MARINADE

½ tbsp garlic and ginger paste

1 fresh green chilli, deseeded and
chopped

1 tsp ground coriander

1 tsp ground cumin

½ tsp ground turmeric

¼–½ tsp chilli powder

1 tbsp water

salt

To make the marinade, mix the garlic and ginger paste, green chilli, ground coriander, cumin, turmeric and chilli powder together with salt to taste in a large bowl. Gradually stir in the water to form a thin paste. Add the fish chunks and smear with the marinade. Tuck the bay leaves underneath and leave to marinate in the refrigerator for at least 30 minutes, or up to 4 hours.

When you are ready to cook the fish, remove from the refrigerator 15 minutes in advance. Melt the ghee in a wok or large frying pan over a medium–high heat. Add the onions, sprinkle with the salt and cook, stirring frequently, for 8 minutes, or until they are very soft and golden.

Gently add the fish with its marinade and the bay leaves to the pan and stir in the water. Bring to the boil, then immediately reduce the heat and cook the fish for 4–5 minutes, spooning the sauce over the fish and carefully moving the chunks around, until they are cooked through and the flesh flakes easily. Adjust the seasoning, if necessary, garnish with coriander and serve with Indian bread.

COOK'S TIP

Do not over-brown the onions or the dish will taste bitter. They should be golden, but not brown, when the fish is added.

Thai Green Fish Curry

The warm waters of Thailand's coastal regions are a rich source of fish and seafood. White fish is a popular addition to many curries as it soaks up the flavours of the sauce and cooks in no time at all.

SERVES 4

2 tbsp vegetable oil

1 garlic clove, chopped

2 tbsp Thai green curry paste

1 small aubergine, diced

125 ml/4 fl oz coconut milk

2 tbsp fish sauce

1 tsp sugar

225 g/8 oz firm white fish fillets,
   cut into pieces

125 ml/4 fl oz fish stock

2 kaffir lime leaves, finely shredded

about 15 fresh Thai basil leaves

fresh dill sprigs, to garnish

Heat the oil in a large frying pan or preheated wok over a medium heat until almost smoking. Add the garlic and cook until golden. Add the curry paste and stir-fry for a few seconds before adding the aubergine. Stir-fry for about 4–5 minutes, until soft.

Add the coconut milk, bring to the boil and stir until it thickens and curdles slightly. Add the fish sauce and sugar to the frying pan and stir well.

Add the fish pieces and stock. Simmer for 3–4 minutes, stirring occasionally, until the fish is just tender. Add the lime leaves and basil, then cook for a further minute. Transfer to a warmed serving dish and garnish with dill sprigs. Serve immediately.

Bengali-style Fish

Fresh fish is eaten a great deal in Bengal (Bangladesh) and this dish is made with mustard oil, which gives the fish a mouth-watering flavour. The mustard plant flourishes in the hot and humid eastern plains surrounding Bengal, and the resulting oil and seeds are used extensively in Asian cooking.

SERVES 4-8

1 tsp ground turmeric

1 tsp salt

1 kg/2 lb 4 oz white fish fillets, such as cod, monkfish, plaice or halibut, skinned and cut into pieces

6 tbsp mustard oil

4 fresh green chillies

1 tsp finely chopped fresh ginger

1 tsp crushed garlic

2 onions, finely chopped

2 tomatoes, finely chopped

450 ml/16 fl oz water

chopped fresh coriander, to garnish

Indian bread, to serve

Mix the turmeric and salt together in a small bowl, then spoon the mixture over the fish pieces.

Heat the oil in a large heavy-based frying pan. Add the fish and cook until pale yellow. Remove the fish with a slotted spoon and reserve.

Place the chillies, ginger, garlic, onions and tomatoes in a mortar and grind with a pestle to make a paste. Alternatively, place the ingredients in a food processor and process until smooth.

Transfer the spice paste to a clean frying pan and dry-fry until golden brown.

Remove the frying pan from the heat and place the fish pieces in the paste without breaking up the fish. Return the frying pan to the heat, add the water and cook over a medium heat for 15–20 minutes. Transfer to a warmed serving dish, garnish with chopped coriander and serve with Indian bread.

Fish in Coconut

Fish and seafood play an important role in Thai cuisine, with many regions having their own specialities. If you like seafood, you will love this appetizing dish, which combines delicate white fish with tender squid and juicy prawns.

SERVES 4

2 tbsp vegetable or groundnut oil

6 spring onions, roughly chopped

2.5-cm/1-inch piece fresh ginger, grated

2–3 tbsp Thai red curry paste

400 ml/14 fl oz coconut milk

150 ml/5 fl oz fish stock

4 kaffir lime leaves

1 lemon grass stalk, broken in half

350 g/12 oz white fish fillets, skinned
    and cut into chunks

225 g/8 oz squid rings and tentacles

225 g/8 oz large cooked peeled prawns

1 tbsp fish sauce

2 tbsp Thai soy sauce

4 tbsp snipped fresh Chinese chives

cooked jasmine rice with chopped fresh
    coriander, to serve

Heat the oil in a wok or large frying pan and stir-fry the spring onions and ginger for 1–2 minutes. Add the curry paste and stir-fry for 1–2 minutes.

Add the coconut milk, fish stock, lime leaves and lemon grass. Bring to the boil, then lower the heat and simmer for 1 minute.

Add the fish, squid and prawns and simmer for 2–3 minutes, until the fish is cooked. Add the fish sauce and soy sauce and stir in the chives. Serve immediately accompanied by cooked jasmine rice with chopped coriander stirred through it.

Goan-style Seafood Curry

With mustard seeds, curry leaves and a creamy coconut sauce, this quick and easy dish could have originated anywhere in southern India, not just in tropical Goa on the west coast. Coconut is a very common ingredient in Goan cooking and both the flesh and milk are used in sweet and savoury dishes.

SERVES 4-6

3 tbsp vegetable or groundnut oil

1 tbsp black mustard seeds

12 fresh or 1 tbsp dried curry leaves

6 shallots, finely chopped

1 garlic clove, crushed

1 tsp ground turmeric

½ tsp ground coriander

¼–½ tsp chilli powder

140 g/5 oz creamed coconut, grated
   and dissolved in 300 ml/10 fl oz
   boiling water

500 g/1 lb 2 oz skinless, boneless white
   fish, such as monkfish or cod, cut into
   large chunks

450 g/1 lb large raw prawns, peeled and
   deveined

finely grated rind and juice of 1 lime

salt

Heat the oil in a wok or large frying pan over a high heat. Add the mustard seeds and stir them around for about 1 minute, or until they pop. Stir in the curry leaves.

Add the shallots and garlic and stir for about 5 minutes, or until the shallots are golden. Stir in the turmeric, coriander and chilli powder and continue stirring for about 30 seconds.

Add the dissolved creamed coconut. Bring to the boil, then reduce the heat to medium and stir for about 2 minutes.

Reduce the heat to low, add the fish and simmer for 1 minute, spooning the sauce over the fish and very gently stirring it around. Add the prawns and continue to simmer for a further 4–5 minutes, until the fish flakes easily and the prawns turn pink and curl.

Add half the lime juice, then taste and add more lime juice and salt to taste. Sprinkle with the lime rind and serve.

Mixed Seafood Curry

This curry is a seafood-lover's dream, combining beneficial oil-rich fish with succulent prawns, tender squid and mouth-watering mussels in an aromatic coconut sauce. Serve with lime wedges for squeezing over.

SERVES 4

1 tbsp vegetable or groundnut oil

3 shallots, finely chopped

2.5-cm/1-inch piece fresh galangal, peeled and thinly sliced

2 garlic cloves, finely chopped

400 ml/14 fl oz coconut milk

2 lemon grass stalks, snapped in half

4 tbsp fish sauce

2 tbsp chilli sauce

225 g/8 oz raw tiger prawns, peeled and deveined

225 g/8 oz baby squid, cleaned and thickly sliced

225 g/8 oz salmon fillet, skinned and cut into chunks

175 g/6 oz tuna steak, cut into chunks

225 g/8 oz fresh mussels, scrubbed and debearded

lime wedges, to garnish

cooked rice, to serve

Heat the oil in a large wok with a tight-fitting lid and stir-fry the shallots, galangal and garlic for 1–2 minutes, until they start to soften. Add the coconut milk, lemon grass, fish sauce and chilli sauce. Bring to the boil, lower the heat and simmer for 1–2 minutes.

Add the prawns, squid, salmon and tuna and simmer for 3–4 minutes, until the prawns have turned pink and the fish is cooked.

Discard any mussels with broken shells or any that refuse to close when tapped with a knife. Add the remaining mussels to the wok and cover with a lid. Simmer for 1–2 minutes, until they have opened. Discard any mussels that remain closed. Garnish with lime wedges and serve immediately with cooked rice.

Fish in Tomato & Chilli Sauce with Fried Onion

This delicious dish, in which firm-fleshed fish is shallow-fried until browned, then simmered in an alluringly spiced chilli and tomato sauce, originates from north-east India. It is best served with plain boiled rice.

SERVES 4

700 g/1 lb 9 oz tilapia fillets, cut into
    5-cm/2-inch pieces

2 tbsp lemon juice

1 tsp salt, or to taste

1 tsp ground turmeric

4 tbsp sunflower or olive oil,
    plus extra for shallow-frying

2 tsp granulated sugar

1 large onion, finely chopped

2 tsp ginger purée

2 tsp garlic purée

½ tsp ground fennel seeds

1 tsp ground coriander

½–1 tsp chilli powder

175 g/6 oz canned chopped tomatoes

300 ml/10 fl oz warm water

2–3 tbsp chopped fresh coriander leaves

cooked basmati rice, to serve

Lay the fish in a large plate and gently rub in the lemon juice, ½ teaspoon of the salt and ½ teaspoon of the turmeric. Set aside for 15–20 minutes.

Pour enough oil for shallow-frying to cover the base of a 23-cm/9-inch frying pan to a depth of about 1 cm/½ inch and place over a medium–high heat. When the oil is hot, fry the pieces of fish, in a single layer, until well browned on both sides and a light crust is formed. Drain on kitchen paper.

Heat the 4 tablespoons of oil in a medium saucepan or frying pan over a medium heat and add the sugar. Allow it to brown, watching it carefully because once it browns it will blacken quickly. As soon as the sugar is brown, add the onion and cook for 5 minutes, until soft. Add the ginger and garlic purées, and cook for a further 3–4 minutes, or until the mixture begins to brown.

Add the ground fennel, ground coriander, chilli powder and the remaining turmeric. Cook for about a minute, then add half the tomatoes. Stir and cook until the tomato juice has evaporated, then add the remaining tomatoes. Continue to cook, stirring, until the oil separates from the spice paste.

Pour in the warm water and add the remaining salt. Bring to the boil and reduce the heat to medium. Add the fish, stir gently, and reduce the heat to low. Cook, uncovered, for 5–6 minutes, then stir in half the chopped coriander and remove from the heat. Serve garnished with the remaining coriander and accompanied by cooked basmati rice.

Fish Korma

Contrary to general belief, korma is not a dish but one of the techniques used in Indian cooking. Fish korma is easy to cook and has an inviting appearance as well as an irresistible aroma and taste.

SERVES 4

700 g/1 lb 9 oz tilapia fillets, cut into
    5-cm/2-inch pieces

1 tbsp lemon juice

1 tsp salt

55 g/2 oz raw unsalted cashews

3 tbsp sunflower or olive oil

5-cm/2-inch piece cinnamon stick,
    halved

4 green cardamom pods, bruised

2 cloves

1 large onion, finely chopped

1–2 fresh green chillies, chopped
    (deseeded if you like)

2 tsp ginger purée

2 tsp garlic purée

150 ml/5 fl oz single cream

55 g/2 oz whole milk natural yogurt

¼ tsp ground turmeric

½ tsp sugar

1 tbsp toasted flaked almonds, to garnish

Indian bread or cooked basmati rice,
    to serve

Place the fish in a large plate and gently rub in the lemon juice and ½ teaspoon of the salt. Set aside for 20 minutes. Soak the cashews in boiling water for 15 minutes.

Heat the oil in a wide shallow pan over a low heat and add the cinnamon, cardamom and cloves. Let them sizzle for 30–40 seconds.

Add the onion, chillies, and ginger and garlic purées. Increase the heat slightly and cook, stirring frequently, for 9–10 minutes, until the onion is very soft.

Meanwhile, drain the cashews and purée them with the cream and yogurt.

Stir the turmeric into the onion mixture and add the puréed ingredients, the remaining salt and the sugar. Mix thoroughly and arrange the fish in the sauce in a single layer. Bring to a slow simmer, cover the pan and cook for 5 minutes. Remove the lid and shake the pan gently from side to side. Spoon some of the sauce over the pieces of fish. Re-cover and cook for a further 3–4 minutes. Transfer to a serving dish and garnish with the toasted almonds. Serve with Indian bread or cooked basmati rice.

Fish in Spicy Coconut Broth

Known as moh hin gha, *this is Burma's national dish, without which no festival is complete. Hawkers carry all the ingredients and a container of charcoal fire across a bamboo pole to cook moh hin gha during festivals and fairs. Moh hin gha is served with an assortment of accompaniments, such as rice noodles, fish cakes, fried chillies, chopped onions and any kind of fritters. It is an ideal dinner party dish.*

SERVES 6

450 g/1 lb tilapia fillets

700 ml/1¼ pints hot water

1 lemon grass stalk

5-cm/2-inch piece fresh ginger

5–6 shallots or 1 large onion, roughly
    chopped

2 fresh red chillies, roughly chopped
    (deseeded if you like)

4 large garlic cloves, roughly chopped

4 tbsp groundnut oil

1 tsp ground turmeric

1 tsp shrimp paste

1 tbsp fish sauce

500 g/1 lb 2 oz canned bamboo shoots
    in water

400 ml/14 fl oz coconut milk

salt

TO SERVE

200 g/7 oz rice noodles, cooked
    according to the instructions on the
    packet

4 hard-boiled eggs

8 dried red chillies, fried in a little oil
    until slightly blackened

4 spring onions (white part only),
    chopped

lime or lemon wedges (optional)

fish cakes or fritters

Put the fish in a large saucepan and pour in the hot water. Slice half the lemon grass and half the ginger and add to the fish. Roughly chop the remaining lemon grass and ginger and set aside. Bring to the boil, reduce the heat to low and simmer for 5–6 minutes. Switch off the heat, cover the pan and leave the ginger and lemon grass to infuse in the stock for 15–20 minutes.

Meanwhile, put the shallots, red chillies, garlic, the remaining lemon grass and the remaining ginger in a food processor or blender and blend until mushy.

Heat the oil in a large saucepan over a medium heat and add the shallot mixture and turmeric and cook, stirring regularly, for 10–12 minutes, reducing the heat for the last few minutes of cooking. Sprinkle over a little water, if necessary, to prevent the mixture from sticking.

Strain the reserved fish stock, reserving the tilapia, and add enough water to make it up to 700 ml/1¼ pints. Pour into the pan along with the shrimp paste and fish sauce. Leave over a low heat while you prepare the bamboo shoots. Drain the bamboo shoots and chop into bite-sized pieces, then add to the pan with the coconut milk. Add salt to taste; both the shrimp paste and the fish sauce are salty so make sure to taste before adding salt.

Break up the tilapia fillets into small pieces and add to the pan. Simmer, uncovered, for 5–6 minutes.

To serve, place the noodles in a bowl and top it up with the broth. Serve all the other accompaniments separately so everyone can help themselves.

Penang Fish Curry

Malaysian fish and seafood curries are very popular all over South East Asia. This recipe, from Penang in western Malaysia, is a delicious combination of spices such as shallots, red chillies, ginger and turmeric. A characteristic ingredient in Malaysian cooking is the candle nut, but since these are only available in Asian stores, this recipe uses roasted peanuts instead to enrich, thicken and add a nutty taste to the sauce.

SERVES 4

25 g/1 oz dry roasted peanuts

8–10 shallots or 2 onions, roughly
   chopped

2–3 fresh red chillies, roughly chopped

2.5-cm/1-inch piece fresh ginger, roughly
   chopped

4 large garlic cloves, roughly chopped

1 tsp shrimp paste

4 tbsp groundnut oil

1 tsp ground turmeric

½ tsp chilli powder

425 ml/15 fl oz warm water

½ tsp salt, or to taste

2 tbsp tamarind juice

½ tsp sugar

700 g/1 lb 9 oz trout fillets, cut into
   1-cm/½-inch slices

fresh coriander sprigs, to garnish

cooked basmati rice, to serve

Put the peanuts, shallots, chilles, ginger, garlic and shrimp paste in a food processor or blender and blend until the mixture is mushy. Remove and set aside.

Heat the oil in a large shallow pan, preferably non-stick, and add the peanut mixture, turmeric and chilli powder. Cook over a medium heat, stirring regularly, until the mixture begins to brown, then continue to cook until the mixture is fragrant, adding a little water from time to time to prevent the mixture from sticking to the base of the pan. This process will take 10–12 minutes.

Pour in the warm water and add the salt, tamarind juice and sugar. Stir and mix well and carefully add the fish. Stir gently to ensure that the fish is covered with the sauce. Cover the pan, reduce the heat to low and cook for 8–10 minutes. Remove from the heat and serve garnished with coriander sprigs and accompanied by cooked basmati rice.

Tandoori Prawns

Quick and easy, this is one of the ways large tiger prawns are cooked in ramshackle-looking beach shacks along the Goan coast. Locals and tourists alike stroll along the sandy beaches and stop for just-cooked fish and shellfish served the way it always should be: ultra-fresh and simply cooked.

SERVES 4

4 tbsp natural yogurt

2 fresh green chillies, deseeded and chopped

½ tbsp garlic and ginger paste

seeds from 4 green cardamom pods

2 tsp ground cumin

1 tsp tomato purée

¼ tsp ground turmeric

¼ tsp salt

pinch of chilli powder, ideally Kashmiri chilli powder

24 raw tiger prawns, thawed if frozen, peeled, deveined and tails left intact

oil, for greasing

lemon or lime wedges, to serve

Put the yogurt, chillies and garlic and ginger paste in a small food processor or spice grinder and whizz until a paste forms. Transfer the paste to a large non-metallic bowl and stir in the cardamom seeds, cumin, tomato purée, turmeric, salt and chilli powder.

Add the prawns to the bowl and use your hands to make sure they are coated with the yogurt marinade. Cover the bowl with clingfilm and chill for at least 30 minutes, or up to 4 hours.

When you are ready to cook, heat a large griddle or frying pan over a high heat until a few drops of water 'dance' when they hit the surface. Use crumpled kitchen paper or a pastry brush to very lightly grease the hot pan with oil.

Use tongs to lift the prawns out of the marinade, letting the excess drip back into the bowl, then place the prawns on the griddle and cook for 2 minutes. Flip the prawns over and cook for a further 1–2 minutes, until they turn pink, curl and are opaque all the way through when you cut one. Serve immediately with lemon or lime wedges for squeezing over.

COOK'S TIP

The spiced yogurt mixture also makes an excellent marinade for tandoori seafood kebabs. Cut 750 g/1 lb 10 oz thick white fish fillets, such as cod, halibut or monkfish, into 4-cm/1½-inch cubes and put into the marinade with 12 or 16 large peeled and deveined prawns. Leave to marinate for at least 30 minutes, or up to 4 hours. Thread the fish and prawns onto 6 greased metal skewers, alternating with pieces of blanched red or green peppers and/or button mushrooms. Cook under a preheated grill for about 15 minutes, turning the skewers and brushing with any leftover marinade frequently, until the fish flakes and the edges of the fish are lightly charred.

Prawn Biryani

This tantalizing dish is packed with warming, aromatic spices and tinged golden with saffron. Biryani dishes can be time-consuming to prepare, but this cheat's version is perfect for supper in a hurry.

SERVES 8

1 tsp saffron strands

55 ml/2 fl oz warm water

2 shallots, roughly chopped

3 garlic cloves, crushed

1 tsp chopped fresh ginger

2 tsp coriander seeds

½ tsp black peppercorns

2 cloves

seeds from 2 green cardamom pods

½ cinnamon stick

1 tsp ground turmeric

1 fresh green chilli, chopped

½ tsp salt

2 tbsp ghee

1 tsp black mustard seeds

500 g/1 lb 2 oz raw tiger prawns, peeled and deveined

300 ml/10 fl oz coconut milk

300 ml/10 fl oz natural yogurt

cooked basmati rice, to serve

toasted flaked almonds and sliced spring onions, to garnish

Soak the saffron in the warm water for 10 minutes. Put the shallots, garlic, ginger, coriander seeds, peppercorns, cloves, cardamom seeds, cinnamon stick, turmeric, chilli and salt into a spice grinder or mortar and grind to a paste.

Melt the ghee in a saucepan and add the mustard seeds. When they start to pop, add the prawns and stir over a high heat for 1 minute. Stir in the spice mix, then the coconut milk and yogurt. Simmer for 20 minutes.

Spoon the prawn mixture into serving bowls. Top with the cooked basmati rice and drizzle over the saffron water. Serve, garnished with the flaked almonds and spring onions.

Prawn Pooris

This restaurant favourite is easy to recreate at home. The deep-fried pooris aren't difficult to make (see page 194 for the recipe), but remember to leave enough time for the dough to rest for 20 minutes before it is fried. Serve this as a starter or main course or make mini pooris and serve the prawn mixture as a dip.

SERVES 6

2 tsp coriander seeds

½ tsp black peppercorns

1 large garlic clove, crushed

1 tsp ground turmeric

¼–½ tsp chilli powder

½ tsp salt

40 g/1½ oz ghee or 3 tbsp vegetable or groundnut oil

1 onion, grated

800 g/1 lb 12 oz canned crushed tomatoes

pinch of sugar

500 g/1 lb 2 oz small cooked peeled prawns, thawed if frozen

½ tsp garam masala, plus extra to garnish

6 pooris, kept warm

fresh chopped coriander, to garnish

Put the coriander seeds, peppercorns, garlic, turmeric, chilli powder and salt in a small food processor, spice grinder or mortar and blend to a thick paste.

Melt the ghee in a wok or large frying pan over a medium–low heat. Add the paste and cook, stirring constantly, for about 30 seconds.

Add the grated onion and stir around for a further 30 seconds. Stir in the tomatoes and the sugar. Bring to the boil, stirring, and leave to bubble for 10 minutes, mashing the tomatoes against the side of the pan to break them down, or until reduced. Taste and add extra salt, if necessary.

Add the prawns and sprinkle with the garam masala. When the prawns are hot, arrange the hot pooris on plates and top each one with a portion of the prawns. Sprinkle with the coriander and garam masala and serve.

COOK'S TIP

Deep-fried pooris are best served straight from the pan, so it is a good idea to have a couple of pans to use if you are entertaining. The pooris, with their rich, light texture, are traditional with this dish, but chapatis or naans are also good, especially if you want to avoid last-minute deep-frying.

Coconut Prawns with Chillies & Curry Leaves

This chilli-spiked, turmeric-tinged prawn curry is mellowed with coconut milk and distinctively flavoured with curry leaves, which are available fresh in Asian shops and dried in large supermarkets. Fresh ones can be frozen for up to three months.

SERVES 4

4 tbsp sunflower or olive oil

½ tsp black or brown mustard seeds

½ tsp fenugreek seeds

1 large onion, finely chopped

2 tsp garlic purée

2 tsp ginger purée

1–2 fresh green chillies, chopped (deseeded if you like)

1 tbsp ground coriander

½ tsp ground turmeric

½ tsp chilli powder

1 tsp salt, or to taste

250 ml/9 fl oz coconut milk

450 g/1 lb cooked peeled tiger prawns, thawed if frozen

1 tbsp tamarind juice or juice of ½ lime

½ tsp crushed black peppercorns

10–12 fresh or dried curry leaves

Heat 3 tablespoons of the oil in a medium saucepan over a medium–high heat. When hot, but not smoking, add the mustard seeds, followed by the fenugreek seeds and the onion. Cook, stirring frequently, for 5–6 minutes, until the onion is soft but not brown. Add the garlic and ginger purées and the chillies and cook, stirring frequently, for a further 5–6 minutes, until the onion is a light golden colour.

Add the coriander, turmeric and chilli powder and cook, stirring, for 1 minute. Add the salt and coconut milk, followed by the prawns and tamarind juice. Bring to a slow simmer and cook, stirring occasionally, for 3–4 minutes.

Meanwhile, heat the remaining 1 tablespoon of oil in a very small saucepan over a medium heat. Add the peppercorns and curry leaves. Turn off the heat and leave to sizzle for 20–25 seconds, then fold the aromatic oil into the prawn mixture. Remove from the heat and serve immediately.

Chilli Prawns with Garlic Noodles

Here is a hot and spicy dish for those chilli enthusiasts! The crunchy mangetout and beansprouts complement the hot flavours well.

SERVES 4

200 g/7 oz cooked peeled king or
 tiger prawns
4 tbsp sweet chilli sauce
4 tbsp groundnut or vegetable oil
4 spring onions, chopped
55 g/2 oz mangetout, trimmed and
 halved diagonally
1 tbsp Thai red curry paste
400 ml/14 fl oz coconut milk
55 g/2 oz canned, drained
 bamboo shoots
55 g/2 oz fresh beansprouts

GARLIC NOODLES

115 g/4 oz dried medium
 egg noodles
2 garlic cloves, crushed
handful of fresh coriander, chopped

Toss the prawns with the chilli sauce in a bowl. Cover and set aside.

Heat half the oil in a preheated wok, add the spring onions and mangetout and stir-fry over a medium–high heat for 2–3 minutes. Add the curry paste and stir well. Pour in the coconut milk and bring gently to the boil, stirring occasionally. Add the bamboo shoots and beansprouts and cook, stirring, for 1 minute. Stir in the prawns and chilli sauce, reduce the heat and simmer for 1–2 minutes, until just heated through.

Meanwhile, cook the noodles in a saucepan of lightly salted boiling water for 4–5 minutes, until just tender, or according to the packet instructions. Drain and return to the saucepan.

Heat the remaining oil in a small non-stick frying pan, add the garlic and stir-fry over a high heat for 30 seconds. Add to the drained noodles with half the coriander and toss together until well mixed.

Transfer the garlic noodles to serving bowls, top with the prawn mixture and serve immediately, garnished with the remaining coriander.

Prawns with Spring Onions & Straw Mushrooms

Straw mushrooms are widely used in Asian cooking and take their name from the paddy straw on which they are grown. Canned straw mushrooms are available from Asian stores.

SERVES 4

2 tbsp vegetable or groundnut oil

bunch of spring onions, chopped

2 garlic cloves, finely chopped

175 g/6 oz creamed coconut, roughly
   chopped

2 tbsp Thai red curry paste

450 ml/16 fl oz fish stock

2 tbsp fish sauce

2 tbsp Thai soy sauce

6 fresh Thai basil sprigs

400 g/14 oz canned straw mushrooms,
   drained

350 g/12 oz large cooked peeled prawns

cooked jasmine rice, to serve

Heat the oil in a wok and stir-fry the spring onions and garlic for 2–3 minutes. Add the creamed coconut, curry paste and stock and heat gently until the coconut has dissolved.

Stir in the fish sauce and soy sauce, then add the basil, mushrooms and prawns. Gradually bring to the boil and serve immediately with cooked jasmine rice.

Goan Prawn Curry with Hard-boiled Eggs

Goa, on the west coast of India, has a cuisine rich in culture and religion. The influence of not only the indigenous Hindu faith, but also Islam and Christianity, both of which came with foreign invaders, has placed Goan cuisine in a unique position. In this recipe, large prawns and hard-boiled eggs are bathed in rich, aromatic coconut milk.

SERVES 4

4 tbsp sunflower or olive oil

1 large onion, finely chopped

2 tsp ginger purée

2 tsp garlic purée

2 tsp ground coriander

½ tsp ground fennel

½ tsp ground turmeric

½–1 tsp chilli powder

½ tsp pepper

2–3 tbsp water

125 g/4½ oz canned chopped tomatoes

200 ml/7 fl oz coconut milk

1 tsp salt, or to taste

4 hard-boiled eggs

700 g/1 lb 9 oz cooked peeled tiger prawns

juice of 1 lime

2–3 tbsp chopped fresh coriander leaves

cooked basmati rice, to serve

Heat the oil in a medium saucepan over a medium–high heat and add the onion. Cook until the onion is soft but not brown. Add the ginger and garlic purées and cook for 2–3 minutes.

In a small bowl, mix the ground coriander, ground fennel, turmeric, chilli powder and pepper. Add the water and make a paste. Reduce the heat to medium, add this paste to the onion mixture and cook for 1–2 minutes. Reduce the heat to low and continue to cook for 3–4 minutes.

Add half the tomatoes and cook for 2–3 minutes. Add the remaining tomatoes and cook for a further 2–3 minutes.

Add the coconut milk and salt, bring to a slow simmer and cook, uncovered, for 6–8 minutes, stirring regularly.

Meanwhile, shell the eggs and, using a sharp knife, make 4 slits lengthways on each egg without cutting them through. Add the eggs to the pan along with the prawns. Increase the heat slightly and cook for 6–8 minutes.

Stir in the lime juice and half the coriander. Remove from the heat and transfer the curry to a serving dish. Garnish with the reserved coriander and serve with cooked basmati rice.

Mussels with Mustard Seeds & Shallots

Baskets piled high with fresh mussels are not an uncommon slight along India's southern Malabar coast. Quickly cooked, fragrant dishes coloured with golden turmeric such as this are served in the open-air restaurants along Kochi's harbourside, opposite the picturesque fishing nets.

SERVES 4

2 kg/4 lb 8 oz live mussels, scrubbed and debearded

3 tbsp vegetable or groundnut oil

½ tbsp black mustard seeds

8 shallots, chopped

2 garlic cloves, crushed

2 tbsp distilled vinegar

4 small fresh red chillies

85 g/3 oz creamed coconut, dissolved in 300 ml/10 fl oz boiling water

10 fresh or 1 tbsp dried curry leaves

½ tsp ground turmeric

¼–½ tsp chilli powder

salt

Discard any mussels with broken shells or any that refuse to close when tapped with a knife. Set aside.

Heat the oil in a wok or large frying pan over a medium–high heat. Add the mustard seeds and stir them around for about 1 minute, or until they start to pop.

Add the shallots and garlic and cook, stirring frequently, for 3 minutes, or until they start to brown. Stir in the vinegar, whole chillies, dissolved creamed coconut, curry leaves, turmeric, chilli powder and a pinch of salt and bring to the boil, stirring.

Reduce the heat to very low. Add the mussels, cover the pan and leave the mussels to simmer, shaking the pan frequently, for 3–4 minutes, or until they are all open. Discard any mussels that remain closed. Ladle the mussels into deep bowls, then taste the broth and add extra salt, if necessary. Spoon over the mussels and serve.

COOK'S TIP

Taste the bright yellow broth before you add it to the serving bowls with the mussels. If the mussels were gritty, strain the liquid through a sieve lined with muslin or kitchen paper. Mussels should be cooked on the day of purchase.

Vegetables & Pulses

Vegetable Korma

The korma style of cooking was originally used only for meat and poultry. However, its popularity is so overwhelming that various vegetarian recipes have been created in recent years. The dish is a subtle sensation of flavours and a total visual delight.

SERVES 4

85 g/3 oz raw cashew nuts

175 ml/6 fl oz boiling water

good pinch of saffron threads, pounded

2 tbsp hot milk

1 small cauliflower, divided into
  1-cm/½-inch florets

115 g/4 oz green beans, cut into
  2.5-cm/1-inch lengths

115 g/4 oz carrots, cut into
  2.5-cm/1-inch sticks

250 g/9 oz new potatoes, boiled in their
  skins and cooled

4 tbsp sunflower or olive oil

1 large onion, finely chopped

2 tsp ginger purée

1–2 fresh green chillies, chopped
  (deseeded if you like)

2 tsp ground coriander

½ tsp ground turmeric

6 tbsp warm water

400 ml/14 fl oz good-quality vegetable
  stock

½ tsp salt, or to taste

2 tbsp single cream

2 tsp ghee or butter

1 tsp garam masala

¼ tsp grated nutmeg

Soak the cashew nuts in the boiling water in a heatproof bowl for 20 minutes. Meanwhile, soak the pounded saffron in the hot milk. Blanch the vegetables, one at a time, in a saucepan of boiling salted water: blanch the cauliflower for 3 minutes, drain and immediately plunge in cold water; blanch the green beans for 3 minutes, drain and plunge in cold water; and blanch the carrots for 4 minutes, drain and plunge in cold water. Peel the potatoes, if you like, and halve or quarter them according to their size.

Heat the oil in a medium heavy-based saucepan over a medium heat. Add the onion, ginger purée and chillies and cook, stirring frequently, for 5–6 minutes, until the onion is soft. Add the coriander and turmeric and cook, stirring, for 1 minute. Add 3 tablespoons of the warm water and cook for 2–3 minutes. Add the remaining warm water, then cook, stirring frequently, for 2–3 minutes, or until the oil separates from the spice paste.

Add the stock, saffron and milk mixture and salt, and bring to the boil. Drain the vegetables, add to the saucepan and return to the boil. Reduce the heat to low and simmer for 2–3 minutes. Meanwhile, put the cashew nuts and their soaking water in a food processor and process until well blended. Add to the korma, then stir in the cream. Leave over a very low heat while you prepare the final seasoning.

Melt the ghee in a very small saucepan over a low heat. Add the garam masala and nutmeg and leave the spices to sizzle gently for 20–25 seconds. Fold the spiced butter into the korma. Remove from the heat and serve immediately.

COOK'S TIP

You can store this korma in the refrigerator for 3–4 days, but reheat very gently, adding a little warm water to maintain the consistency of the sauce.

Vietnamese Vegetable Curry

Curries are popular in South Vietnam, where Indian-influenced spicy foods are enjoyed. This vegetable and tofu curry can be served with French baguette (the classic way), rice or noodles.

SERVES 6

2 lemon grass stalks

50 ml/2 fl oz vegetable oil

3 large garlic cloves, crushed

1 large shallot, thinly sliced

2 tbsp Indian curry powder

700 ml/1¼ pints coconut milk

500 ml/18 fl oz coconut water (not
  coconut milk) or vegetable stock

2 tbsp fish sauce

4 fresh red bird's eye chillies or dried red
  Chinese (tien sien) chillies

6 kaffir lime leaves

1 carrot, peeled and cut diagonally into
  1 cm/½ inch thick pieces

1 small–medium Asian aubergine,
  cut into 2.5-cm/1-inch pieces

1 small–medium bamboo shoot, cut into
  thin wedges

115 g/4 oz sugar snap peas, trimmed

12 large shiitake mushrooms, stems
  discarded, caps halved

450 g/1 lb firm or extra-firm tofu,
  drained and cut into 2.5-cm/1-inch
  cubes

fresh chopped coriander and fried
  shallots, to garnish

Discard the bruised leaves and root ends of the lemon grass stalks, then slice 15–20 cm/6–8 inches of the lower stalks paper thin.

Heat the oil in a large saucepan over a high heat, add the garlic and shallot and stir-fry for 5 minutes, or until golden. Add the lemon grass and curry powder and stir-fry for 2 minutes, or until fragrant. Add the coconut milk, coconut water, fish sauce, chillies and lime leaves and bring to the boil. Reduce the heat to low, then add the carrot and aubergine, cover and cook for 10 minutes.

Add the bamboo shoot, sugar snap peas, mushrooms and tofu and cook for a further 5 minutes.

Serve garnished with the coriander and fried shallots

COOK'S TIP

Boiled and vacuum-packed whole bamboo shoots from Japan are the best. These can be sliced and used without any further preparation. If using fresh bamboo, be sure to peel and boil the shoot for 10 minutes in water before using in the recipe. If using frozen raw bamboo, do the same. If using canned bamboo, make sure to use a whole shoot instead of precut shoots. Bamboo shoots have the ability to absorb flavour. For this reason, canned bamboo must be boiled for 2 minutes to eliminate any flavour from the can.

Carrot & Pumpkin Curry

This creamy carrot and pumpkin curry, with its gorgeous autumnal colours, is perfect comfort food. It would be equally delicious made with butternut squash instead of the pumpkin.

SERVES 4

150 ml/5 fl oz vegetable stock

2.5-cm/1-inch piece fresh galangal, sliced

2 garlic cloves, chopped

1 lemon grass stalk (white part only), finely chopped

2 fresh red chillies, deseeded and chopped

4 carrots, peeled and cut into chunks

225 g/8 oz pumpkin, peeled, deseeded and cut into cubes

2 tbsp vegetable or groundnut oil

2 shallots, finely chopped

3 tbsp Thai yellow curry paste

400 ml/14 fl oz coconut milk

4–6 fresh Thai basil sprigs

25 g/1 oz toasted pumpkin seeds, to garnish

Pour the stock into a large saucepan and bring to the boil. Add the galangal, half the garlic, the lemon grass and chillies and simmer for 5 minutes. Add the carrots and pumpkin and simmer for 5–6 minutes, until tender.

Meanwhile, heat the oil in a wok or frying pan and stir-fry the shallots and the remaining garlic for 2–3 minutes. Add the curry paste and stir-fry for 1–2 minutes.

Stir the shallot mixture into the saucepan and add the coconut milk and Thai basil. Simmer for 2–3 minutes. Serve hot, sprinkled with the toasted pumpkin seeds.

Vegetables with Tofu & Spinach

Tofu has been a staple protein in many parts of Asia for many centuries and is renowned for its ability to absorb whatever flavouring it is mixed with. Here it is deep-fried until crisp and used as a topping for a creamy Thai-style vegetable curry.

SERVES 4

vegetable or groundnut oil,
  for deep-frying

225 g/8 oz firm tofu, drained and
  cut into cubes

2 tbsp vegetable or groundnut oil

2 onions, chopped

2 garlic cloves, chopped

1 fresh red chilli, deseeded and sliced

3 celery sticks, diagonally sliced

225 g/8 oz mushrooms, thickly sliced

115 g/4 oz baby corn cobs, cut in half

1 red pepper, deseeded and cut into
  strips

3 tbsp Thai red curry paste

400 ml/14 fl oz coconut milk

1 tsp palm sugar or soft light brown
  sugar

2 tbsp Thai soy sauce

225 g/8 oz baby spinach leaves

Heat the oil for deep-frying in a preheated wok, deep saucepan or deep-fat fryer to 180–190°C/350–375°F, or until a cube of bread browns in 30 seconds. Add the tofu cubes, in batches, and cook for 4–5 minutes, until crisp and brown all over. Remove with a slotted spoon and drain on kitchen paper.

Heat the 2 tablespoons of oil in a wok or frying pan and stir-fry the onions, garlic and chilli for 1–2 minutes, until they start to soften. Add the celery, mushrooms, corn cobs and red pepper and stir-fry for 3–4 minutes, until they soften.

Stir in the curry paste and coconut milk and gradually bring to the boil. Add the sugar and soy sauce and then the spinach. Cook, stirring constantly, until the spinach has wilted. Serve immediately, topped with the tofu.

Red Curry with Mixed Leaves

This eye-catching mixture of green shoots and leaves should be cooked quickly to retain the varied textures of the ingredients.

SERVES 4

2 tbsp groundnut or vegetable oil

2 onions, thinly sliced

1 bunch of fine asparagus spears

400 ml/14 fl oz coconut milk

2 tbsp Thai red curry paste

3 fresh kaffir lime leaves

225 g/8 oz baby spinach leaves

2 heads pak choi, chopped

1 small head Chinese leaves, shredded

handful of fresh coriander, chopped

cooked rice, to serve

Heat the oil in a preheated wok, add the onions and asparagus and stir-fry over a medium–high heat for 1–2 minutes.

Add the coconut milk, curry paste and lime leaves and bring gently to the boil, stirring occasionally. Add the spinach, pak choi and Chinese leaves and cook, stirring, for 2–3 minutes, until wilted. Add the coriander and stir well. Serve immediately with rice.

COOK'S TIP

For non-vegetarians, scatter some shredded or diced cooked chicken or cooked peeled prawns over the cooked rice to accompany the curry.

Cauliflower, Aubergine & Green Bean Korma

Mild and fragrant, this slow-braised mixed vegetable dish reflects the skilled flavouring of Mogul cooking. The rich, almost velvety, cream-based sauce is spiced but doesn't contain chillies, making it an indulgent treat for anyone who prefers mild dishes.

SERVES 4-6

85 g/3 oz cashew nuts

1½ tbsp garlic and ginger paste

200 ml/7 fl oz water

55 g/2 oz ghee or 4 tbsp vegetable
  or groundnut oil

1 large onion, chopped

5 green cardamom pods, bruised

1 cinnamon stick, broken in half

¼ tsp ground turmeric

250 ml/9 fl oz double cream

140 g/5 oz new potatoes, scrubbed and
  chopped into 1-cm/½-inch pieces

140 g/5 oz cauliflower florets

½ tsp garam masala

140 g/5 oz aubergine, chopped into
  2.5-cm/1-inch chunks

140 g/5 oz green beans, chopped into
  2.5-cm/1-inch lengths

salt and pepper

chopped fresh mint or coriander,
  to garnish

Heat a large flameproof casserole or frying pan with a tight-fitting lid over a high heat. Add the cashew nuts and stir them around until they start to brown, then immediately tip them out of the casserole.

Put the nuts in a spice blender with the garlic and ginger paste and 1 tablespoon of the water and whizz until a coarse paste forms.

Melt half the ghee in the casserole over a medium–high heat. Add the onion and cook for 5–8 minutes, until golden brown.

Add the nut paste and stir for 5 minutes. Stir in the cardamom pods, cinnamon stick and turmeric.

Add the cream and the remaining water and bring to the boil, stirring. Reduce the heat to the lowest level, cover the casserole and simmer for 5 minutes.

Add the potatoes, cauliflower and garam masala and simmer, covered, for 5 minutes. Stir in the aubergine and green beans and continue simmering for a further 5 minutes, or until all the vegetables are tender. Check the sauce occasionally to make sure it isn't sticking on the base of the pan, and stir in a little water if needed.

Taste and add seasoning, if necessary. Sprinkle with the mint or coriander and serve.

COOK'S TIP
When you serve this, remember to tell guests that it contains cardamom pods, which have a bitter taste if bitten into.

Broccoli with Peanuts

This innovative dish combines fragrant spices with tender vegetables and is perfect for making broccoli more appealing. The tasty topping of crunchy peanuts adds texture and interest.

SERVES 4

3 tbsp vegetable or groundnut oil

1 lemon grass stalk, roughly chopped

2 fresh red chillies, deseeded and chopped

2.5-cm/1-inch piece fresh ginger, grated

3 kaffir lime leaves, roughly torn

3 tbsp Thai green curry paste

1 onion, chopped

1 red pepper, deseeded and chopped

350 g/12 oz broccoli, cut into florets

115 g/4 oz fine French beans

55 g/2 oz unsalted peanuts

Put 2 tablespoons of the oil, the lemon grass, chillies, ginger, lime leaves and curry paste into a food processor or blender and process to a paste.

Heat the remaining oil in a wok, add the spice paste, onion and red pepper and stir-fry for 2–3 minutes, until the vegetables start to soften.

Add the broccoli and French beans, cover and cook over a low heat, stirring occasionally, for 4–5 minutes, until tender.

Meanwhile, toast or dry-fry the peanuts until lightly browned. Add them to the broccoli mixture and toss together. Serve immediately.

Okra Stir-fried with Onions

Okra stir-fried with onions and spices makes a superb side dish. Here, the combination of the soft green okra, bright red pepper and white onion, all dotted with black mustard seeds, creates a colourful, appetizing effect.

SERVES 4

280 g/10 oz okra

1 small red pepper

1 onion

2 tbsp sunflower or olive oil

1 tsp black or brown mustard seeds

½ tsp cumin seeds

3 large garlic cloves, lightly crushed, then chopped

½ tsp chilli powder

½ tsp salt, or to taste

½ tsp garam masala

cooked basmati rice, to serve

Scrub each okra gently, rinse well in cold running water, then slice off the hard head. Halve diagonally and set aside.

Remove the seeds and core from the red pepper and cut into 4-cm/1-inch strips. Halve the onion lengthways and cut into 5 mm/¼ inch thick slices.

Heat the oil in a heavy-based frying pan or wok over a medium heat. When hot but not smoking, add the mustard seeds, followed by the cumin seeds. Remove from the heat and add the garlic. Return to a low heat and cook the garlic gently, stirring, for 1 minute, or until lightly browned.

Add the okra, red pepper and onion, increase the heat to medium–high and stir-fry for 2 minutes. Add the chilli powder and salt and stir-fry for a further 3 minutes. Add the garam masala and stir-fry for 1 minute. Remove from the heat and serve immediately with cooked basmati rice.

COOK'S TIP

Make sure that the oil is at the right temperature or else the mustard seeds will not release their delightful nutty taste. To test the temperature, drop 1–2 mustard seeds into the hot oil – if they pop straight away, the oil is just right.

Vegetables in a Creamy Tomato Sauce

There is nothing better to accompany an Asian meal than a selection of fresh vegetables in a lightly spiced sauce. The choice of the combination of vegetables can be completely flexible, but remember to choose them with visual appeal in mind. Here, carrots, potatoes and green beans are used to create a colourful appearance.

SERVES 4

200 g/7 oz fresh green beans, cut into 5-cm/2-inch lengths

200 g/7 oz cauliflower, divided into 1-cm/½-inch florets

200 g/7 oz baby carrots, peeled and left whole

200 g/7 oz boiled potatoes

4 tbsp sunflower or olive oil

5 green cardamom pods, bruised

2 bay leaves

1 large onion, finely chopped

2.5-cm/1-inch piece fresh ginger, finely grated

1 tsp ground coriander

½ tsp ground cumin

1 tsp ground turmeric

½–1 tsp chilli powder

1 tbsp tomato purée

1 tsp salt, or to taste

150 ml/5 fl oz warm water

150 ml/5 fl oz double cream

2 tomatoes, deseeded and roughly chopped

Indian bread or cooked basmati rice, to serve

Blanch all the vegetables separately (the green beans will need 3 minutes; the cauliflower 3 minutes; and the carrots 5 minutes) and plunge them in cold water. Cut the potatoes into 2.5-cm/1-inch cubes.

Heat the oil in a medium saucepan over a low heat and add the cardamom and bay leaves. Allow them to sizzle for 30–40 seconds, then add the onion and ginger. Increase the heat to medium and cook for 5–6 minutes, until the onion is soft, stirring regularly.

Add the coriander, cumin, turmeric and chilli powder. Cook for 2–3 minutes, then add a little water and continue to cook for a further minute. Add the tomato purée and cook for about a minute.

Drain the green beans, cauliflower and carrots, and add to the pan along with the potatoes. Add the salt, stir and pour in the warm water. Cook, uncovered, for 2–3 minutes, then add the cream. Cook for 3–4 minutes, fold in the tomatoes and remove from the heat. Serve with Indian bread or cooked basmati rice.

Cumin-scented Aubergine & Potato Curry

Chunks of aubergine, with its beautiful shiny skin, and creamy potatoes are cooked in a richly spiced tomato and onion sauce that is aromatized with nigella seeds and intensified with fresh chillies. A delicious, healthy dish to enjoy with any Indian bread.

SERVES 4

1 large aubergine, about 350 g/12 oz

225 g/8 oz potatoes, boiled in their skins
   and cooled

3 tbsp sunflower or olive oil

½ tsp black mustard seeds

½ tsp nigella seeds

½ tsp fennel seeds

1 onion, finely chopped

2.5-cm/1-inch piece fresh ginger, grated

2 fresh green chillies, chopped
   (deseeded if you like)

½ tsp ground cumin

1 tsp ground coriander

1 tsp ground turmeric

½ tsp chilli powder

1 tbsp tomato purée

450 ml/15 fl oz warm water

1 tsp salt, or to taste

½ tsp garam masala

2 tbsp chopped fresh coriander leaves

Indian bread, to serve

Quarter the aubergine lengthways and cut the stem end of each quarter into 5-cm/2-inch pieces. Halve the remaining part of each quarter and cut into the same size as above. Soak the aubergine pieces in cold water.

Peel the potatoes and cut into into 5-cm/2-inch cubes. Heat the oil in a large saucepan over a medium heat. When hot, add the mustard seeds and, as soon as they start popping, add the nigella seeds and fennel seeds.

Add the onion, ginger and chillies and cook for 7–8 minutes, until the mixture begins to brown.

Add the cumin, coriander, turmeric and chilli powder. Cook for about a minute, then add add the tomato purée. Cook for a further minute, pour in the warm water, then add the salt and aubergine. Bring to the boil and cook over a medium heat for 8–10 minutes, stirring frequently to ensure that the aubergine cooks evenly. At the start of cooking, the aubergine will float, but once it soaks up the liquid it will sink quite quickly. As soon as the aubergine sinks, add the potatoes and cook for 2–3 minutes, stirring.

Stir in the garam masala and chopped coriander and remove from the heat. Serve with Indian bread.

Mushroom Bhaji

Mushroom bhaji is not a traditional Indian dish, but mushrooms do seem to have a certain affinity with a spiced tomato-based sauce. It is important to choose the right combination of spices in order to complement the natural taste of the mushrooms.

SERVES 4

280 g/10 oz closed-cup white
    mushrooms
4 tbsp sunflower or olive oil
1 onion, finely chopped
1 fresh green chilli, finely chopped
    (deseeded if you like)
2 tsp garlic purée
1 tsp ground cumin
1 tsp ground coriander
½ tsp chilli powder
½ tsp salt, or to taste
1 tbsp tomato purée
3 tbsp water
1 tbsp snipped fresh chives, to garnish

Wipe the mushrooms with damp kitchen paper and thickly slice.

Heat the oil in a medium saucepan over a medium heat. Add the onion and chilli and cook, stirring frequently, for 5–6 minutes, until the onion is soft but not brown. Add the garlic purée and cook, stirring, for 2 minutes.

Add the cumin, coriander and chilli powder and cook, stirring, for 1 minute. Add the mushrooms, salt and tomato purée and stir until all the ingredients are thoroughly blended.

Sprinkle the water evenly over the mushrooms and reduce the heat to low. Cover and cook for 10 minutes, stirring halfway through. The sauce should have thickened, but if it appears runny, cook, uncovered, for 3–4 minutes, or until you achieve the desired consistency.

Transfer to a serving dish, sprinkle the chives on top and serve immediately.

Garden Peas & Paneer in Chilli-tomato Sauce

Paneer, or Indian cheese, is a great source of protein for the vast majority of the Indian population who don't eat meat. This is a traditional vegetarian main course where tender morsels of paneer are simmered in a spice-infused tomato sauce.

SERVES 4

4 tbsp sunflower or olive oil

250 g/9 oz paneer, cut into
    2.5-cm/1-inch cubes

4 green cardamom pods, bruised

2 bay leaves

1 onion, finely chopped

2 tsp garlic purée

2 tsp ginger purée

2 tsp ground coriander

½ tsp ground turmeric

½–1 tsp chilli powder

150 g/5½ oz canned chopped tomatoes

425 ml/15 fl oz warm water,
    plus 2 tbsp

1 tsp salt, or to taste

125 g/4½ oz frozen peas

½ tsp garam masala

2 tbsp single cream

2 tbsp chopped fresh coriander leaves

Indian bread, to serve

Heat 2 tablespoons of the oil in a medium non-stick saucepan over a medium heat. Add the paneer and cook, stirring frequently, for 3–4 minutes, or until evenly browned. Paneer tends to splatter in hot oil, so stand slightly away from the hob. Alternatively, use a splatter screen. Remove and drain on kitchen paper.

Add the remaining oil to the saucepan and reduce the heat to low. Add the cardamom pods and bay leaves and leave to sizzle gently for 20–25 seconds. Add the onion, increase the heat to medium and cook, stirring frequently, for 4–5 minutes, until the onion is soft. Add the garlic and ginger purées and cook, stirring frequently, for a further 3–4 minutes, until the onion is a pale golden colour.

Add the ground coriander, turmeric and chilli powder and cook, stirring, for 1 minute. Add the tomatoes and cook, stirring frequently, for 4–5 minutes. Add the 2 tablespoons of warm water and cook, stirring frequently, for 3 minutes, or until the oil separates from the spice paste.

Add the remaining warm water and the salt. Bring to the boil, then reduce the heat to low and simmer, uncovered, for 7–8 minutes.

Add the paneer and peas and simmer for 5 minutes. Stir in the garam masala, cream and chopped coriander and remove from the heat. Serve immediately with Indian bread.

Garlic & Chilli Potatoes with Cauliflower

Known as aloo gobi, *this is a well-known and popular dish in most Indian restaurants. There are as many different versions as there are cooks. This version is easy to make, can be part-prepared ahead of time and is deliciously moreish!*

SERVES 4

350 g/12 oz new potatoes

1 small cauliflower

2 tbsp sunflower or olive oil

1 tsp black or brown mustard seeds

1 tsp cumin seeds

5 large garlic cloves, lightly crushed, then chopped

1–2 fresh green chillies, finely chopped (deseeded if you like)

½ tsp ground turmeric

½ tsp salt, or to taste

2 tbsp chopped fresh coriander leaves

Indian bread, to serve

Cook the potatoes in their skins in a saucepan of boiling water for 20 minutes, or until tender. Drain, then soak in cold water for 30 minutes. Peel them, if you like, then halve or quarter according to their size – they should be a similar size to the cauliflower florets (see below).

Meanwhile, divide the cauliflower into about 1-cm/½-inch florets and blanch in a large saucepan of boiling salted water for 3 minutes. Drain and plunge into iced water to prevent further cooking, then drain again.

Heat the oil in a medium saucepan over a medium heat. When hot, but not smoking, add the mustard seeds, then the cumin seeds.

Remove from the heat and add the garlic and chillies. Return to a low heat and cook, stirring, until the garlic has a light brown tinge.

Stir in the turmeric, followed by the cauliflower and the potatoes. Add the salt, increase the heat slightly and cook, stirring, until the vegetables are well blended with the spices and heated through.

Stir in the coriander, remove from the heat and serve immediately with Indian bread.

Potatoes with Spiced Spinach

This traditional and popular dish is easy to make and is a perfect accompaniment to most Indian meals. Generally, fresh spinach leaves are blanched and puréed, but you can use frozen puréed spinach, which cuts down on preparation time.

SERVES 4

350 g/12 oz new potatoes

250 g/9 oz spinach leaves, thawed
   if frozen

3 tbsp sunflower or olive oil

1 large onion, finely sliced

1 fresh green chilli, finely chopped
   (deseeded if you like)

2 tsp garlic purée

2 tsp ginger purée

1 tsp ground coriander

½ tsp ground cumin

½ tsp chilli powder

½ tsp ground turmeric

200 g/7 oz canned chopped tomatoes

½ tsp granulated sugar

1 tsp salt, or to taste

3 tbsp single cream

Cook the potatoes in their skins in a saucepan of boiling water for 20 minutes, or until tender. Drain, then soak in cold water for 30 minutes. Peel them, if you like, then halve or quarter according to their size. Meanwhile, blanch the spinach in a large saucepan of boiling salted water for 2 minutes, then drain. Transfer to a blender or food processor and blend to a purée. Set aside.

Heat 2 tablespoons of the oil in a medium saucepan over a medium heat. Add the onion and cook, stirring frequently, for 10–12 minutes, until well browned, reducing the heat to low for the last 2–3 minutes. Remove from the heat and remove the excess oil from the onion by pressing against the side of the saucepan with a wooden spoon. Remove and drain on kitchen paper.

Return the pan to the heat, add the remaining oil and heat. Add the chilli and garlic and ginger purées and cook over low heat, stirring, for 2–3 minutes. Add the coriander, cumin, chilli powder and turmeric and cook, stirring, for 1 minute. Add the tomatoes, increase the heat to medium and add the sugar. Cook, stirring frequently, for 5–6 minutes, until the tomatoes have reached a paste-like consistency.

Add the potatoes, spinach, salt and fried onions and cook, stirring, for 2–3 minutes. Stir in the cream and cook for 1 minute. Remove from the heat and serve immediately.

Chickpeas in Coconut Milk

From the palm-fringed southern coastal area of India, where coconut milk is used as an everyday stock, this is a simple but delicious dish. Traditionally, dried chickpeas would be used, but canned chickpeas are a quick and easy alternative.

SERVES 4

275 g/9¾ oz potatoes, cut into
   1-cm/½-inch cubes

250 ml/9 fl oz hot water

400 g/14 oz canned chickpeas, drained
   and rinsed

250 ml/9 fl oz coconut milk

1 tsp salt, or to taste

2 tbsp sunflower or olive oil

4 large garlic cloves, finely chopped
   or crushed

2 tsp ground coriander

½ tsp ground turmeric

½–1 tsp chilli powder

juice of ½ lemon

Indian bread or cooked basmati rice,
   to serve

Put the potatoes in a medium saucepan and pour in the hot water. Bring to the boil, then reduce the heat to low and cook, covered, for 6–7 minutes. Add the chickpeas and cook, uncovered, for 3–4 minutes, until the potatoes are tender.

Add the coconut milk and salt and bring to a slow simmer.

Meanwhile, heat the oil in a small saucepan over a low heat. Add the garlic and cook, stirring frequently, until it begins to brown. Add the coriander, turmeric and chilli powder and cook, stirring, for 25–30 seconds.

Fold the aromatic oil into the chickpeas. Stir in the lemon juice and remove from the heat. Serve immediately with Indian bread or cooked basmati rice.

COOK'S TIP

You can use green beans or a mixture of green beans and carrots instead of the potatoes. Black-eyed beans are also excellent for this recipe.

Spiced Black-eyed Beans & Mushrooms

This is a combination made in heaven – tender black-eyed beans with their earthy, nutty taste combine extremely well with the mildly earthy mushrooms, which absorb the flavours of the spices beautifully.A rich, red tomato sauce with flecks of emerald green mint shows off the creamy beans and mushrooms like a pretty picture.

SERVES 4

1 onion, roughly chopped

4 large garlic cloves, roughly chopped

2.5-cm/1-inch piece fresh ginger, roughly chopped

4 tbsp sunflower or olive oil

1 tsp ground cumin

1 tsp ground coriander

½ tsp ground fennel

1 tsp ground turmeric

½–1 tsp chilli powder

175 g/6 oz canned chopped tomatoes

400 g/14 oz canned black-eyed beans, drained and rinsed

115 g/4 oz large flat mushrooms, wiped and cut into bite-sized pieces

½ tsp salt, or to taste

175 ml/6 fl oz warm water

1 tbsp chopped fresh mint

1 tbsp chopped fresh coriander leaves

1 small tomato, deseeded and cut into julienne strips, to garnish

Indian bread, to serve

Purée the onion, garlic and ginger in a food processor or blender.

Heat the oil in a medium saucepan over a medium heat and add the puréed ingredients. Cook for 4–5 minutes, then add the cumin, ground coriander, ground fennel, turmeric and chilli powder. Stir-fry for about a minute, then add the tomatoes. Cook until the tomatoes are pulpy and the juice has evaporated.

Add the black-eyed beans, mushrooms and salt. Stir well and pour in the warm water, bring to the boil, cover the pan and reduce the heat to low. Simmer for 8–10 minutes, stirring halfway through.

Stir in the chopped mint and coriander and remove from the heat. Transfer to a serving dish and garnish with the strips of tomato. Serve as a main course with Indian bread or as an accompaniment to meat, fish or poultry dishes.

Lentils with Fresh Chillies, Mint & Coriander

This recipe is characteristic of the cooking of the Punjab in north India; like the people of this state, the cooking is robust, lively and full of character. Two types of lentils are first sautéed with aromatic spices and simmered until tender. Traditionally, a type of lentil known as urad dhal is used, which you can buy from Indian stores, but this recipe uses red split lentils as they are more readily available. Serve it with any Indian bread.

SERVES 4

85 g/3 oz red split lentils (masoor dhal)

85 g/3 oz skinless split chickpeas
    (channa dhal)

3 tbsp sunflower or olive oil

1 onion, finely chopped

2–3 fresh green chillies, chopped
    (deseeded if you like)

2 tsp garlic purée

2 tsp ginger purée

1 tsp ground cumin

600 ml/1 pint warm water

1 tsp salt, or to taste

1 tbsp chopped fresh mint

1 tbsp chopped fresh coriander leaves

55 g/2 oz unsalted butter

1 fresh green chilli and 1 small tomato,
    deseeded and cut into julienne strips,
    to garnish

Wash the lentils and chickpeas together until the water runs clear and leave to soak for 30 minutes.

Heat the oil in a medium saucepan, preferably non-stick, over a medium heat and add the onion, chillies and garlic and ginger purées. Stir-fry the mixture until it begins to brown.

Drain the lentils and chickpeas and add to the onion mixture together with the cumin. Reduce the heat to low and stir-fry for 2–3 minutes, then pour in the warm water. Bring to the boil, reduce the heat to low, cover and simmer 25–30 minutes.

Stir in the salt, mint, fresh coriander and butter. Stir until the butter has melted, then remove from the heat. Serve garnished with the strips of chilli and tomato.

Mixed Lentils with Five-spice Seasoning

The Bengali five-spice seasoning panch phoran *is a typical combination of whole spices used in East and North East India. As you will see from the ingredients list below, they are all whole spices and are highly aromatic. A winning combination of yellow mung beans and red split lentils (known as* mung dhal *and* masoor dhal*) is used here. The golden lentils, boldly patterned with chopped tomatoes and fresh green coriander and dotted with black mustard and nigella seeds, look quite stunning and taste delicious.*

SERVES 4

125 g/4½ oz red split lentils
(masoor dhal)

125 g/4½ oz skinless split mung beans
(mung dhal)

900 ml/1½ pints hot water

1 tsp ground turmeric

1 tsp salt, or to taste

1 tbsp lemon juice

2 tbsp sunflower or olive oil

¼ tsp black mustard seeds

¼ tsp cumin seeds

¼ tsp nigella seeds

¼ tsp fennel seeds

4–5 fenugreek seeds

2–3 dried red chillies

1 small tomato, deseeded and cut into
strips, and fresh coriander sprigs,
to garnish

Indian bread, to serve

Mix both types of lentils together and wash until the water runs clear. Put them into a saucepan with the hot water. Bring to the boil and reduce the heat slightly. Let it boil for 5–6 minutes, and when the foam subsides, add the turmeric, reduce the heat to low, cover and cook for 20 minutes. Add the salt and lemon juice and beat the dhal with a wire beater. Add a little more hot water if the dhal is too thick.

Heat the oil in a small saucepan over a medium heat. When hot, but not smoking, add the mustard seeds. As soon as they begin to pop, reduce the heat to low and add the cumin seeds, nigella seeds, fennel seeds, fenugreek seeds and dried chillies. Let the spices sizzle until the seeds begin to pop and the chillies have blackened. Pour the contents of the saucepan over the lentils, scraping off every bit from the saucepan.

Turn off the heat and keep the saucepan covered until you are ready to serve. Transfer to a serving dish and garnish with tomato strips and coriander sprigs. Serve as a main course with Indian bread or as an accompaniment to meat, fish or poultry dishes.

Lentils with Cumin & Shallots

This dish, traditionally known as tarka dhal, *is easy to cook. The word* tarka *means 'tempering' – the boiled dhal is tempered with a few whole spices, and chopped shallots are added to the hot oil before being folded into the cooked lentils.*

SERVES 4

200 g/7 oz red split lentils

850 ml/1½ pints water

1 tsp salt, or to taste

2 tsp sunflower or olive oil

½ tsp black or brown mustard seeds

½ tsp cumin seeds

4 shallots, finely chopped

2 fresh green chillies, chopped
  (deseeded if you like)

1 tsp ground turmeric

1 tsp ground cumin

1 fresh tomato, chopped

2 tbsp chopped fresh coriander leaves

Wash the lentils until the water runs clear and put into a medium saucepan. Add the water and bring to the boil. Reduce the heat to medium and skim off the foam. Cook, uncovered, for 10 minutes. Reduce the heat to low, cover and cook for 45 minutes, stirring occasionally to ensure that the lentils do not stick to the base of the pan as they thicken. Stir in the salt.

Meanwhile, heat the oil in a small saucepan over a medium heat. When hot, but not smoking, add the mustard seeds, followed by the cumin seeds. Add the shallots and chillies and cook, stirring, for 2–3 minutes, then add the turmeric and ground cumin. Add the tomato and cook, stirring, for 30 seconds.

Fold the shallot mixture into the cooked lentils. Stir in the coriander, remove from the heat and serve immediately.

COOK'S TIP
If you add salt too soon to the lentils, they will take longer to cook.

Egg & Lentil Curry

This egg and lentil curry is an excellent source of protein for vegetarians. The lentils soak up the flavours of the spices beautifully. Chapattis (see page 188 for the recipe) make an excellent accompaniment to this dish.

SERVES 4

3 tbsp ghee or vegetable oil

1 large onion, chopped

2 garlic cloves, chopped

2.5-cm/1-inch piece fresh ginger, chopped

½ tsp minced chilli or chilli powder

1 tsp ground coriander

1 tsp ground cumin

1 tsp paprika

85 g/3 oz split red lentils

450 ml/16 fl oz vegetable stock

225 g/8 oz canned chopped tomatoes

6 eggs

55 ml/2 fl oz coconut milk

2 tomatoes, cut into wedges

salt

fresh coriander sprigs, to garnish

chapattis, to serve

Melt the ghee in a saucepan, add the onion and cook gently for 3 minutes. Stir in the garlic, ginger, chilli and spices and cook gently, stirring frequently, for 1 minute. Stir in the lentils, stock and tomatoes and bring to the boil. Reduce the heat, cover and simmer, stirring occasionally, for 30 minutes, until the lentils are tender.

Meanwhile, place the eggs in a saucepan of cold water and bring to the boil. Reduce the heat and simmer for 10 minutes. Drain and cover immediately with cold water.

Stir the coconut milk into the lentil mixture and season well with salt. Process the mixture in a blender or food processor until smooth. Return to the pan and heat through.

Shell the hard-boiled eggs and cut into quarters. Divide the hard-boiled egg quarters and tomato wedges between serving plates. Spoon over the hot lentil sauce and garnish with coriander sprigs. Serve hot with chapattis.

Accompaniments

Chapattis

In Indian homes, chapattis are made fresh every day, using a special flour known as atta. *Asian stores sell atta, but you can substitute a fine wholemeal bread flour combined with plain flour, at a ratio of two-thirds wholemeal to one-third plain.*

MAKES 16

400 g/14 oz chapatti flour (atta),
  plus extra for dusting
1 tsp salt
½ tsp granulated sugar
2 tbsp sunflower or olive oil
250 ml/9 fl oz lukewarm water

Mix the chapatti flour, salt and sugar together in a large bowl. Add the oil and work well into the flour mixture with your fingertips. Gradually add the water, mixing at the same time. When the dough is formed, transfer to a work surface and knead for 4–5 minutes. The dough is ready when all the excess moisture is absorbed by the flour. Alternatively, mix the dough in a food processor. Wrap the dough in clingfilm and leave to rest for 30 minutes.

Divide the dough in half, then cut each half into 8 equal-sized pieces. Form each piece into a ball and flatten into a round cake. Dust each cake lightly in the flour and roll out to a 15-cm/6-inch round. Keep the remaining cakes covered while you are working on one. The chapattis will cook better when freshly rolled out, so roll out and cook one at a time.

Preheat a heavy-based cast-iron griddle or a large heavy-based frying pan over a medium–high heat. Put a chapatti on the griddle and cook for 30 seconds. Using a fish slice, turn over and cook until bubbles begin to appear on the surface. Turn over again. Press the edges down gently with a clean cloth to encourage the chapatti to puff up – they will not always puff up, but this doesn't matter. Cook until brown patches appear on the underside. Remove from the pan and keep hot by wrapping in a piece of foil lined with kitchen paper. Repeat with the remaining dough cakes.

Chilli-coriander Naan

Naan came to India with the ancient Persians, and it means 'bread' in their language. Naan is traditionally made in a clay tandoor oven, but this can be emulated by using a very hot grill.

MAKES 8

450 g/1 lb plain flour

2 tsp sugar

1 tsp salt

1 tsp baking powder

1 egg

250 ml/9 fl oz milk

2 tbsp sunflower or olive oil,
   plus extra for oiling

2 fresh red chillies, chopped (deseeded
   if you like)

15 g/½ oz fresh coriander leaves,
   chopped

2 tbsp butter, melted

Sift the flour, sugar, salt and baking powder together into a large bowl. Whisk the egg and milk together and gradually add to the flour mixture, mixing it with a wooden spoon, until a dough is formed.

Transfer the dough to a work surface, make a depression in the centre of the dough and add the oil. Knead for 3–4 minutes, until the oil is absorbed by the flour and you have a smooth and pliable dough. Wrap the dough in clingfilm and leave to rest for 1 hour.

Divide the dough into 8 equal-sized pieces, form each piece into a ball and flatten into a thick cake. Cover the dough cakes with clingfilm and leave to rest for 10–15 minutes.

Preheat the grill to high. Line a grill pan with a piece of foil and brush with oil.

The traditional shape of naan is teardrop, but you can make them any shape you wish. To make the traditional shape, roll each flattened cake into a 13-cm/5-inch round and pull the lower end gently. Carefully roll out again, maintaining the teardrop shape, to about 23 cm/9 inches in diameter. Alternatively, roll the flattened cakes out to 23-cm/9-inch rounds.

Mix the chillies and coriander together, then divide into 8 equal portions and spread each on the surface of a naan. Press gently so that the mixture sticks to the dough. Transfer a naan to the prepared grill pan and cook 13 cm/5 inches below the heat source for 1 minute, or until slightly puffed and brown patches appear on the surface. Watch carefully, and as soon as brown spots appear on the surface, turn over and cook the other side for 45–50 seconds, until lightly browned. Remove from the grill and brush with the melted butter. Wrap in a tea towel while you cook the remaining naans.

Parathas

These are shallow-fried unleavened breads for special occasions and religious festivals. Made with lots of melted ghee, parathas have a flaky texture and are too rich for everyday meals – unless, of course, you don't worry about your waistline! For an Indian-style breakfast, try parathas with a bowl of thick yogurt.

MAKES 8

225 g/8 oz wholemeal flour, sifted,
plus extra for dusting

½ tsp salt

150–200 ml/5–7 fl oz water

140 g/5 oz ghee, melted

Mix the flour and salt together in a large bowl and make a well in the centre. Gradually stir in enough water to make a stiff dough. Turn out the dough onto a lightly floured surface and knead for 10 minutes, or until it is smooth and elastic. Shape the dough into a ball and place it in the cleaned bowl, then cover with a damp tea towel and leave to rest for 20 minutes.

Divide the dough into 8 equal-sized pieces. Lightly flour your hands and roll each piece of dough into a ball. Working with one ball of dough at a time, roll it out on a lightly floured work surface until it is a 13-cm/ 5-inch round. Brush the top of the dough with about 1½ teaspoons of the melted ghee. Fold the round in half to make a half-moon shape and brush the top again with melted ghee. Fold the half-moon shape in half again to make a triangle. Press the layers together.

Roll out the triangle on a lightly floured surface into a larger triangle that is about 18 cm/7 inches on each side. Flip the dough back and forth between your hands a couple of times, then cover with a damp cloth and continue until all the dough is shaped and rolled.

Meanwhile, heat a large ungreased frying pan or griddle over a high heat until very hot and a splash of water 'dances' when it hits the surface. Place a paratha in the pan and cook until bubbles appear on the surface. Flip the paratha over and brush the surface with melted ghee. Continue cooking until the bottom is golden brown, then flip the paratha over again and smear with more melted ghee. Use a fish slice to press down on the surface of the paratha so it cooks evenly.

Brush with more melted ghee and serve, then repeat with the remaining parathas. Parathas are best served as soon as they come out of the pan, but they can be kept warm wrapped in foil for about 20 minutes.

Pooris

These deep-fried breads puff up to look like balloons when they go into the hot oil, and are perfect for serving with most curries. Children love watching these cooking, but do keep them at a safe distance. Pooris are made in huge quantities to serve at Hindu weddings and special occasions.

MAKES 12

225 g/8 oz wholemeal flour, sifted,
plus extra for dusting

½ teaspoon salt

30 g/1 oz ghee, melted

100–150 ml/3½–5 fl oz water

vegetable or groundnut oil,
for deep-frying

Put the flour and salt into a bowl and drizzle the ghee over the surface. Gradually stir in the water until a stiff dough forms.

Turn out the dough onto a lightly floured surface and knead for 10 minutes, or until it is smooth and elastic. Shape the dough into a ball and place it in the cleaned bowl, then cover with a damp tea towel and leave to rest for 20 minutes.

Divide the dough into 12 equal-sized pieces and roll each into a ball. Working with one ball of dough at a time, flatten the dough between your palms, then thinly roll it out on a lightly floured work surface into a 13-cm/5-inch round. Continue until all the dough balls are rolled out.

Heat at least 7.5 cm/3 inches oil in a wok, deep-fat fryer or large frying pan until it reaches 180°C/350°F, or until a cube of bread browns in 30 seconds. Drop one poori into the hot fat and fry for about 10 seconds, or until it puffs up. Use 2 large spoons to flip the poori over and spoon some hot oil over the top.

Use the 2 spoons to lift the poori from the oil and let any excess oil drip back into the pan. Drain the poori on crumpled kitchen paper and serve immediately. Continue until all the pooris are fried, making sure the oil returns to the correct temperature before you add another poori.

COOK'S TIP

To make mini pooris, roll out the dough, then use a lightly greased 4-cm/1½-inch biscuit cutter to stamp out smaller rounds.

Dosas

In southern India, these ultra-thin, crisp pancakes are served with coriander chutney or coconut sambal for snacks, or even rolled around a spicy potato mixture and served for breakfast. As dosas are cooked in a thin layer of ghee, they have a rich flavour. Remember to start on the batter a day in advance because it needs to be left to soak overnight.

MAKES 8

115 g/4 oz basmati rice, rinsed

70 g/2½ oz split black lentils (urad dal chilke)

¼ tsp fenugreek seeds

125 ml/4 fl oz water

30 g/1 oz ghee, melted

salt

Bring a pan of salted water to the boil, add the basmati rice and boil for 5 minutes, then drain. Put the rice, split black lentils and fenugreek seeds in a bowl with water to cover and leave to soak overnight.

The next day, strain the rice and lentils, reserving the soaking liquid. Put the rice and lentils in a food processor with 75 ml/2½ fl oz of the water and whizz until a smooth, sludgy grey paste forms. Slowly add the remaining water.

Cover the bowl with a tea towel that has been soaked in hot water and wrung out and leave to ferment in a warm place for 5–6 hours, until small bubbles appear all over the surface.

Stir the mixture and add as much extra water as necessary to get a consistency of single cream. Add salt to taste. The amount of salt you need depends on how sour-tasting the batter is.

Heat the flattest, largest pan you have over a high heat until a splash of water 'dances' when it hits the surface, then brush the surface with melted ghee. Put a ladleful of batter in the centre of the pan and use the bottom of the ladle to spread it out as thinly as possible, then leave it to cook for 2 minutes, until it is golden brown and crisp on the bottom.

Flip the dosa over and continue cooking for a further 2 minutes. Turn out of the pan and keep warm if you are going to wrap it around a filling, or leave to cool. Continue until all the batter has been used.

COOK'S TIP

Don't be tempted to flip a dosa before it has cooked long enough to become crisp on the bottom. It helps to use the largest, flattest pan you have – a griddle or crêpe pan makes the job easier.

Spiced Basmati Rice

This delicately flavoured dish comes from Rajasthan and has never fallen from favour since the days of Mogul rule. It is excellent to serve with lamb dishes.

SERVES 4-6

225 g/8 oz basmati rice

30 g/1 oz ghee or 2 tbsp vegetable
   or groundnut oil

5 green cardamom pods, bruised

5 cloves

2 bay leaves

½ cinnamon stick

1 tsp fennel seeds

½ tsp black mustard seeds

450 ml/16 fl oz water

1½ tsp salt

2 tbsp chopped fresh coriander

pepper

Rinse the basmati rice in several changes of water until the water runs clear, then leave to soak for 30 minutes. Drain and set aside until ready to cook.

Melt the ghee in a flameproof casserole or large saucepan with a tight-fitting lid over a medium–high heat. Add the spices and stir for 30 seconds. Stir the rice into the casserole so the grains are coated with ghee. Stir in the water and salt and bring to the boil.

Reduce the heat to as low as possible and cover the casserole tightly. Simmer, without lifting the lid, for 8–10 minutes, until the grains are tender and all the liquid is absorbed.

Turn off the heat and use 2 forks to mix in the coriander. Adjust the seasoning, if necessary. Re-cover the pan and leave to stand for 5 minutes.

COOK'S TIP

For spiced saffron basmati rice, lightly toast 1 teaspoon of saffron threads in a dry frying pan over a medium–high heat until you can smell the aroma, then immediately tip them out of the pan. Bring the water to the boil while the rice soaks, stir in the saffron threads and the salt and set aside to infuse. Follow the recipe above, using the saffron-infused water in place of the plain water.

Mint & Coriander Rice with Toasted Pine Kernels

The slender grains of fragrant basmati rice complement the delicately flavoured pine kernels, both prized ingredients from northern India, in this sumptuous pilau. Saffron adds an exotic touch, with its age-old reputation for being rare and costly.

SERVES 4

good pinch of saffron threads, pounded

2 tbsp hot milk

225 g/8 oz basmati rice

2 tbsp sunflower or olive oil

5-cm/2-inch piece cinnamon stick, broken in half

4 green cardamom pods, bruised

2 star anise

2 bay leaves

450 ml/16 fl oz lukewarm water

3 tbsp fresh coriander leaves, finely chopped

2 tbsp fresh mint leaves, finely chopped, or 1 tsp dried mint

1 tsp salt, or to taste

25 g/1 oz pine kernels

Soak the pounded saffron threads in the hot milk and set aside until you are ready to use.

Wash the rice in several changes of cold water until the water runs clear. Leave to soak in fresh cold water for 20 minutes, then leave to drain in a colander.

Heat the oil in a medium heavy-based saucepan over a low heat. Add the cinnamon, cardamom, star anise and bay leaves and leave to sizzle gently for 20–25 seconds. Add the rice and stir well to ensure that the grains are coated with the flavoured oil.

Add the water, stir once and bring to the boil. Add the saffron and milk, coriander, mint and salt and boil for 2–3 minutes. Cover tightly, reduce the heat to very low and cook for 7–8 minutes. Turn off the heat and leave to stand, covered, for 7–8 minutes.

Meanwhile, preheat a small heavy-based frying pan over a medium heat, add the pine kernels and cook, stirring, until they begin to glisten with their natural oils and are lightly toasted. Alternatively, cook in a foil-covered grill pan under a preheated medium grill, turning 2–3 times, until lightly toasted. Transfer to a plate and leave to cool.

Add half the toasted pine kernels to the rice and fluff up the rice with a fork. Transfer to a serving dish, garnish with the remaining pine kernels and serve immediately.

Lemon-laced Basmati Rice

In this much-loved dish from southern India, the snow-white grains of basmati rice are tinged with turmeric and adorned with black mustard seeds. The main flavour here is that of curry leaves, which is the hallmark of southern Indian cuisine.

SERVES 4

225 g/8 oz basmati rice

2 tbsp sunflower or olive oil

½ tsp black or brown mustard seeds

10–12 curry leaves, preferably fresh

25 g/1 oz cashew nuts

¼ tsp ground turmeric

1 tsp salt, or to taste

450 ml/16 fl oz hot water

2 tbsp lemon juice

Wash the rice in several changes of cold water until the water runs clear. Leave to soak in fresh cold water for 20 minutes, then leave to drain in a colander.

Heat the oil in a non-stick saucepan over a medium heat. When hot, but not smoking, add the mustard seeds, followed by the curry leaves and the cashew nuts.

Stir in the turmeric, quickly followed by the rice and salt. Cook, stirring, for 1 minute, then add the hot water and lemon juice. Stir once, bring to the boil and boil for 2 minutes. Cover tightly, reduce the heat to very low and cook for 8 minutes. Turn off the heat and leave to stand, covered, for 6–7 minutes. Fork through the rice and transfer to a serving dish. Serve immediately.

COOK'S TIP

It is important to allow the cooked rice to stand to enable the grains to absorb any remaining moisture. Use a metal spoon to transfer the rice to the serving dish, as a wooden spoon will squash the delicate grains.

Coconut Rice

Regarded as the 'fruit of the gods', coconut plays a major role not only in southern Indian kitchens, but also in Hindu religious ceremonies, where it can be used to symbolize a full, rich life. Fittingly, this dish is ideal for all special occasions.

SERVES 4-6

225 g/8 oz basmati rice

450 ml/16 fl oz water

60 g/2¼ oz creamed coconut

2 tbsp mustard oil

1½ tsp salt

Rinse the basmati rice in several changes of water until the water runs clear, then leave to soak for 30 minutes. Drain and set aside until ready to cook.

Bring the water to the boil in a small saucepan, stir in the creamed coconut until it dissolves and then set aside.

Heat the mustard oil in a large frying pan or saucepan with a lid over a high heat until it smokes. Turn off the heat and leave the mustard oil to cool completely.

When you are ready to cook, reheat the mustard oil over a medium–high heat. Add the rice and stir until all the grains are coated in oil. Add the water with the dissolved coconut and bring to the boil.

Reduce the heat to as low as possible, stir in the salt and cover the pan tightly. Simmer, without lifting the lid, for 8–10 minutes, until the grains are tender and all the liquid is absorbed.

Turn off the heat and use 2 forks to mix the rice. Adjust the seasoning, if necessary. Re-cover the pan and leave the rice to stand for 5 minutes.

COOK'S TIP

The mustard oil is heated and then cooled in order to reduce the pungency of its flavour. If you prefer to use vegetable or groundnut oil, you can skip this step.

Cucumber Raita

Raita is a generic name for any salad with a spiced yogurt dressing. In the north of India, the yogurt is flavoured with roasted crushed cumin seeds and chilli, while southern India excels in making a yogurt dressing with a hot oil seasoning.

SERVES 4-5

1 small cucumber

175 g/6 oz whole milk natural yogurt

¼ tsp granulated sugar

¼ tsp salt

1 tsp cumin seeds

10–12 black peppercorns

¼ tsp paprika

Peel the cucumber and scoop out the seeds. Cut the flesh into bite-sized pieces and set aside.

Put the yogurt in a bowl and beat with a fork until smooth. Add the sugar and salt and mix well.

Preheat a small heavy-based saucepan over a medium–high heat. When the pan is hot, turn off the heat and add the cumin seeds and peppercorns. Stir around for 40–50 seconds, until they release their aroma. Remove from the pan and leave to cool for 5 minutes, then crush in a mortar with a pestle or on a hard surface with a rolling pin.

Reserve ¼ teaspoon of this mixture and stir the remainder into the yogurt. Add the cucumber and stir to mix. Transfer the raita to a serving dish and sprinkle with the reserved toasted spices and the paprika.

COOK'S TIP

To add an extra dimension to the taste and texture of the raita, crush 55 g/2 oz roasted salted peanuts. Mix half into the raita and sprinkle the remainder on top just before serving.

Coriander Chutney

This is an example of one of the uncooked, fresh-tasting chutneys that are served with every meal or snack throughout the day in Kerala, starting with breakfast. The bright green coriander, fresh coconut and chilli capture the flavours of the region.

MAKES 225 G/8 OZ

1½ tbsp lemon juice

1½ tbsp water

85 g/3 oz fresh coriander leaves and stems, roughly chopped

2 tbsp chopped fresh coconut

1 small shallot, very finely chopped

5-mm/¼-inch piece fresh ginger, chopped

1 fresh green chilli, deseeded and chopped

½ tsp sugar

½ tsp salt

pinch of pepper

Put the lemon juice and water in a small food processor, add half the coriander and whizz until it is blended and a slushy paste forms. Gradually add the remaining coriander and whizz until it is all blended, scraping down the sides of the processor, if necessary.

If you don't have a processor that will cope with this small amount, use a pestle and mortar, adding the coriander in small amounts.

Add the remaining ingredients and continue processing until they are all finely chopped and blended. Taste and adjust any of the seasonings, if you like. Transfer to a non-metallic bowl, cover and chill for up to 3 days before serving.

COOK'S TIP

For a cooling coriander raita, stir 300 ml/10 fl oz natural yogurt into the chutney and chill for at least 1 hour. Sprinkle with plenty of chopped fresh coriander just before serving.

Chilli & Onion Chutney

For those who really like spicy hot food, this fresh chutney packs quite a punch. It's hot, zingy and can bring tears to your eyes if you don't deseed the chillies. Gujarati people will include the chilli seeds and serve this at all meals, eating it in the summer like a snack with poppadoms or pooris.

MAKES 225 G/8 OZ

1–2 fresh green chillies, finely chopped
   (deseeded if you like)

1 small fresh bird's eye chilli, finely
   chopped (deseeded if you like)

1 tbsp white wine vinegar or cider
   vinegar

2 onions, finely chopped

2 tbsp fresh lemon juice

1 tbsp sugar

3 tbsp chopped fresh coriander, mint
   or parsley, or a combination of herbs

salt

chilli flower, to garnish

Put the chillies in a small non-metallic bowl with the vinegar, stir around and then drain. Return the chillies to the bowl and stir in the onions, lemon juice, sugar and herbs, then add salt to taste.

Leave to stand at room temperature or cover and chill for 15 minutes. Garnish with the chilli flower before serving.

COOK'S TIP

To make the chilli flower garnish, use a sharp knife to make several cuts lengthways along the chilli, keeping the stem end intact. Put the chilli in a bowl of iced water and let stand for 25–30 minutes, or until the cut edges have spread out to form a flower shape.

Coconut Sambal

Coconuts grow in abundance along the gently flowing backwaters of Kerala, and slightly crunchy fresh chutneys like this are served at many meals. Serve this with poppadoms as a snack or use it as an accompaniment to simply cooked fresh seafood.

MAKES 140 G/5 OZ

½ fresh coconut or 125 g/4½ oz
   desiccated coconut

2 fresh green chillies, chopped
   (deseeded if you like)

2.5-cm/1-inch piece fresh ginger, peeled
   and finely chopped

4 tbsp chopped fresh coriander

2 tbsp lemon juice, or to taste

2 shallots, very finely chopped

If you are using a whole coconut, use a hammer and nail to punch a hole in the 'eye' of the coconut, then pour out the water from the inside and reserve. Use the hammer to break the coconut in half, then peel half and chop.

Put the coconut and chillies in a food processor and process for about 30 seconds, until finely chopped. Add the ginger, coriander and lemon juice and process again.

If the mixture seems too dry, stir in about 1 tablespoon of coconut water or water. Stir in the shallots and serve immediately, or cover and chill until required.

COOK'S TIP

This sambal will keep its fresh flavour for up to 3 days if stored in the refrigerator.

Mango Chutney

This light, spiced chutney is about as far as one can get from the thick, overly sweet mango chutney sold in jars. It adds the sunny flavour of Goa and southern India to any Asian meal.

MAKES 250 G/9 OZ

1 large mango, about 400 g/14 oz,
    peeled, stoned and finely chopped

2 tbsp lime juice

1 tbsp vegetable or groundnut oil

2 shallots, finely chopped

1 garlic clove, finely chopped

2 fresh green chillies, deseeded and
    finely sliced

1 tsp black mustard seeds

1 tsp coriander seeds

5 tbsp palm sugar or soft light brown
    sugar

5 tbsp white wine vinegar

1 tsp salt

pinch of ground ginger

Put the mango in a non-metallic bowl with the lime juice and set aside.

Heat the oil in a large frying pan or saucepan over a medium–high heat. Add the shallots and cook for 3 minutes. Add the garlic and chillies and stir for a further 2 minutes, or until the shallots are soft but not brown. Add the mustard seeds and coriander seeds and then stir around.

Add the mango to the pan with the palm sugar, vinegar, salt and ground ginger and stir around. Reduce the heat to its lowest setting and simmer for 10 minutes, until the liquid thickens and the mango becomes sticky.

Remove from the heat and leave to cool completely. Transfer to an airtight container, cover and chill for 3 days before using.

COOK'S TIP
This chutney should be stored in the refrigerator and used within 1 week.

Tamarind Chutney

There isn't any mistaking the fresh, sour taste of tamarind: it adds a distinctive flavour to many dishes, especially those from southern India. More like a sauce than a thick chutney, this sweet-and-sour tasting mixture is essential to serve with samosas and it also goes particularly well with fried fish.

MAKES 250 G/9 OZ

100 g/3½ oz tamarind pulp, chopped

450 ml/16 fl oz water

½ fresh bird's eye chilli, or to taste, deseeded and chopped

55 g/2 oz soft light brown sugar, or to taste

½ tsp salt, or to taste

Put the tamarind and water in a heavy-based saucepan over a high heat and bring to the boil. Reduce the heat to the lowest setting and simmer for 25 minutes, stirring occasionally to break up the tamarind pulp, or until tender.

Tip the tamarind pulp into a sieve and use a wooden spoon to push the pulp into the rinsed-out pan.

Stir in the chilli, sugar and salt and continue simmering for a further 10 minutes, or until the desired consistency is reached. Leave to cool slightly, then stir in extra sugar or salt, to taste.

Leave to cool completely, then cover tightly and chill for up to 3 days, or freeze.

Lime Pickle

With chunky pieces of lime, mouth-watering spices and lots of zest, this hot and tangy pickle is the perfect accompaniment to a whole range of Asian dishes

MAKES 225 G/8 OZ

12 limes, halved and deseeded

115 g/4 oz salt

70 g/2½ oz chilli powder

25 g/1 oz mustard powder

25 g/1 oz ground fenugreek

1 tbsp ground turmeric

300 ml/10 fl oz mustard oil

15 g/½ oz yellow mustard seeds, crushed

½ tsp asafoetida

Cut each lime half into 4 pieces and pack them into a large sterilized jar, sprinkling over the salt at the same time. Cover and leave to stand in a warm place for 10–14 days, or until the limes have turned brown and softened.

Mix the chilli powder, mustard powder, fenugreek and turmeric together in a small bowl and add to the jar of limes. Stir to mix, then re-cover and leave to stand for 2 days.

Transfer the lime mixture to a heatproof bowl. Heat the mustard oil in a heavy-based frying pan. Add the mustard seeds and asafoetida to the pan and cook, stirring constantly, until the oil is very hot and just beginning to smoke.

Pour the oil and spices over the limes and mix well. Cover and leave to cool. When cool, pack into a sterilized jar, seal and store in a sunny place for 1 week before serving.

COOK'S TIP

If you are planning to serve this hot pickle on a particular occasion, it is best to start preparing it a month in advance. Unlike most Indian chutneys, it cannot be eaten immediately after making.

Index

Award-winning cookery writer Mridula Baljekar is a best-selling author of many Indian cookery books. She was born and raised in North East India and when she moved to England she turned her childhood passion for cooking into a highly successful career.

Mridula presented her own series, 'Mridula's Indian Kitchen', and the highly acclaimed 'Spice Trail' on Carlton Food Network. In India she appeared on the most popular channel NDTV and also Door Darshan. She is regularly invited to present cookery shows on regional and national radio stations such as LBC Radio, BBC Southern Counties, BBC Berkshire, BBC Birmingham and the Food Programme on Radio 4.

She owned a contemporary Indian restaurant in Windsor, Berkshire, England, which won several prestigious awards. Mridula has now sold her award-winning restaurant in order to concentrate on her writing and media career. As well as running highly successful cookery classes, she is developing a range of chutneys and ready meals which she hopes to put on the supermarket shelves very soon.

Mridula's food has been described in the media as 'Heaven on Earth for the senses', 'route to spice heaven', and 'traditional Indian cuisine with a brilliant modern twist'.

Bibliography
Grove, Colleen and Peter. *Curry Culture*. Menu Publications, 2005
Norman, Jill. *Complete Book of Spices*. Dorling Kindersley, 1990.